HOW TO USE CHAT- GPT TO BECOME A SUCCESSFUL ENTREPRENEUR

9 SECRET STEPS WHICH MAKES YOU BILLIONAIRE

PROF. NEHAL AHMAD

NISHAT FATMA

Made with ♥ on the Notion Press Platform
www.notionpress.com

This book is dedicated to the Almighty, whose blessings and guidance have been my source of strength and inspiration throughout this journey. Without His divine grace, none of this would have been possible.

To my parents, your unwavering support and endless love have been the bedrock of my success. Your sacrifices and belief in my dreams have given me the courage to pursue my passions and the resilience to overcome challenges. I owe everything to the values and lessons you have instilled in me.

To my family, thank you for your constant encouragement and understanding. Your patience and support during the countless hours I spent working on this book have been invaluable. You are my greatest source of motivation and joy.

To my friends, your camaraderie, feedback, and encouragement have been indispensable. Your belief in me and my vision has been a driving force behind this project. Thank you for being my pillars of strength and for always standing by my side.

This book is a testament to the collective love, support, and faith of all those who have been a part of my journey. It is with deep gratitude and heartfelt appreciation that I dedicate this work to all of you.

With all my love,

Nehal Ahmad

Contents

FOREWORD

In an age where technology is redefining the boundaries of what's possible, entrepreneurs must stay ahead of the curve to thrive. One such groundbreaking innovation is ChatGPT, an advanced AI language model by OpenAI. This ebook, "How to Use ChatGPT to Become a Successful Entrepreneur: 9 Secret Steps " is a beacon for those ready to harness AI's transformative power.

As someone deeply entrenched in the entrepreneurial world, I've seen firsthand how the right tools and strategies can catapult a business from obscurity to success. ChatGPT represents one of the most potent tools available today. It has the potential to revolutionize customer interactions, automate repetitive tasks, and provide deep insights into market trends—all of which are crucial for scaling a business in today's competitive landscape.

The author of this ebook has distilled their extensive experience and insights into nine actionable steps that any entrepreneur can follow. These steps are not just theoretical constructs but practical guidelines that have been tested and proven in real-world scenarios. They cover a broad spectrum of applications—from enhancing customer service to generating innovative content, from conducting comprehensive market research to crafting personalized marketing campaigns.

What sets this book apart is its accessibility. Whether you're a seasoned business leader or just starting your entrepreneurial journey, you will find the guidance clear, concise, and incredibly valuable. The strategies outlined in these pages are designed to be implemented immediately, providing you with tangible results and a competitive edge.

As you delve into this ebook, I encourage you to approach it with an open mind and a willingness to experiment. The fusion of entrepreneurial spirit and cutting-edge technology is a powerful force. By integrating ChatGPT into your business strategy, you are not just adopting a tool—you are embracing a paradigm shift that can propel you towards unprecedented success.

Prepare to embark on a journey that will not only change the way you do business but also redefine your potential for success. Enjoy the exploration, and here's to your future as a billionaire entrepreneur.

Preface

In today's rapidly evolving digital landscape, the ability to leverage cutting-edge technology can be the difference between success and obscurity. Among the most transformative tools available to entrepreneurs is ChatGPT, an advanced AI language model developed by OpenAI. This ebook, "How to Use ChatGPT to Become a Successful Entrepreneur: 9 Secret Steps " is your definitive guide to harnessing the power of this revolutionary technology. As an entrepreneur, you are constantly seeking innovative ways to enhance your business, streamline operations, and engage with customers. ChatGPT offers unprecedented opportunities to achieve these goals through intelligent automation, personalized customer interactions, and insightful data analysis. Whether you're a startup founder or an established business leader, understanding how to integrate ChatGPT into your strategy can unlock new levels of efficiency and growth. In the following chapters, you will discover nine meticulously curated steps that will guide you through the process of incorporating ChatGPT into your entrepreneurial journey. These steps are not merely theoretical; they are actionable strategies derived from real-world applications and success stories. From automating customer service to generating creative content, and from conducting market research to personalizing marketing campaigns, you will learn how to utilize ChatGPT to its fullest potential.This book is designed for entrepreneurs at all stages, whether you're just starting out or looking to scale your business to new heights. By the end of this guide, you will have a comprehensive understanding of how to leverage ChatGPT to drive innovation, increase productivity, and ultimately, achieve extraordinary financial success.I invite you to embark on this journey with an open mind and a willingness to embrace new technology. Together, we will explore the secrets that can transform your entrepreneurial dreams into reality.

Welcome to a new era of entrepreneurship. Let's get started!

Acknowledgements

Creating "How to Use ChatGPT to Become a Successful Entrepreneur: 9 Secret Steps " has been an incredible journey, and I owe a debt of gratitude to many.

First and foremost, I am deeply grateful to the Almighty for granting me the strength, wisdom, and perseverance to complete this book. Without His guidance and blessings, this journey would not have been possible.

To my parents, your unwavering support and belief in me have been the foundation of my success. Your love, sacrifices, and encouragement have shaped me into the person I am today. Thank you for always standing by me and inspiring me to reach for the stars.

To my family, your patience and understanding during the countless hours I dedicated to this project have been invaluable. Your constant love and support have given me the motivation to keep pushing forward. A special thanks to my wife and co. Author Nishat Fatma , whose faith in my vision has been a driving force.

To my friends, you have been my pillars of strength and my sounding boards throughout this journey. Your encouragement, feedback, and camaraderie have made this process enjoyable and fulfilling. Thank you for believing in me and for your invaluable contributions to this book.

Lastly, to everyone who has supported me in this endeavor, whether directly or indirectly, your impact has been profound. Your encouragement and belief in my vision have helped bring this book to life.

This book is a testament to the collective support, love, and guidance I have received from all of you. I am truly blessed and deeply grateful to have you in my life.

ACKNOWLEDGEMENTS

With heartfelt gratitude,
Nehal Ahmad

Prologue

Imagine a world where the boundaries between human ingenuity and artificial intelligence blur, creating a synergy that propels businesses to unprecedented heights. This is not a vision of a distant future; it is the reality we live in today. At the heart of this transformation is ChatGPT, a groundbreaking AI language model developed by OpenAI, poised to revolutionize the way we conduct business.

In "How to Use ChatGPT to Become a Successful Entrepreneur: 9 Secret Steps Which Make You a Billionaire," you are about to embark on a journey that merges cutting-edge technology with entrepreneurial acumen. This prologue sets the stage for a comprehensive guide that will equip you with the tools and strategies needed to harness the power of ChatGPT, turning innovative ideas into thriving enterprises.

The entrepreneurial landscape is constantly evolving, and staying ahead requires more than just traditional business acumen. It demands an understanding of emerging technologies and the foresight to integrate them effectively. ChatGPT offers a unique advantage, enabling you to streamline operations, enhance customer engagement, and make data-driven decisions with ease.

Throughout the pages of this book, you will uncover nine secret steps designed to transform your entrepreneurial aspirations into tangible success. These steps are not abstract concepts but practical, actionable strategies that have been crafted from real-world experiences and success stories. Whether you are seeking to automate routine tasks, create compelling content, or gain insights into market trends, ChatGPT holds the key.

This book is not just a guide; it is a roadmap to success in the digital age. By embracing the capabilities of ChatGPT, you will unlock new potential within your business, positioning yourself at the forefront of innovation and growth.

As you turn the page and delve into the secrets that follow, prepare to revolutionize your approach to entrepreneurship. Welcome to a world where AI and ambition converge, and where your journey to becoming a billionaire entrepreneur begins.

About The Author

Mr. Nehal Ahmad is a distinguished Engineer and Academician with extensive expertise in Mechanical Engineering. With over 15 years of Teaching Experience, he has trained more than 15,000 students, making significant contributions to their academic and professional development. His industrial experience spans five years, during which he gained valuable insights that he brings into his teaching and research. As a researcher, Mr. Ahmad has more than a decade of experience and has published numerous research papers, establishing himself as a thought leader in his field.

Beyond his academic and research endeavours, Mr. Ahmad is also a certified student coach and career counsellor, dedicated to guiding students in their career paths. His entrepreneurial spirit led him to found Educulate, a venture focused on education and student development, where he has accumulated over 10 years of entrepreneurial experience. Throughout this journey, Mr. Ahmad has honed various skills essential for growing his venture, leveraging cutting-edge technologies such as ChatGPT to enhance his business operations and educational offerings.

Impressed by the capabilities of artificial intelligence, Mr. Ahmad has been inspired to share his entrepreneurial journey and the valuable lessons learned through his experiences. His forthcoming books'HOW To USE CHAT-GPT TO BECOME A SUCCESSFUL ENTREPRENEUR 9-SECRET STEPS ' aim to provide young entrepreneurs with practical insights and strategies, empowering them to navigate their own entrepreneurial paths successfully.

Mr. Nehal Ahmad's multifaceted career reflects a blend of engineering expertise, educational excellence, and innovative entrepreneurship, making him a valuable mentor and guide for aspiring engineers and entrepreneurs.

ABSTRACT

In today's fast-paced business world, staying ahead means embracing the latest technologies. This book, "How to Use ChatGPT to Become a Successful Entrepreneur: 9 Secret Steps is a practical guide to using ChatGPT, a powerful AI tool developed by OpenAI, to transform your business.

This book breaks down nine key steps to help you harness ChatGPT's capabilities. You'll learn how to automate tasks, improve customer service, create engaging content, and make smart, data-driven decisions. These steps are easy to follow and are designed to give you a competitive edge in the market.

Whether you're just starting out or looking to grow your existing business, this book offers valuable insights and practical advice. It is filled with real-world examples and success stories, showing how entrepreneurs like you have used ChatGPT to achieve remarkable results.

The goal of this book is simple: to help you unlock the full potential of ChatGPT and use it to drive your business to new heights. By following the nine secret steps outlined here, you can streamline your operations, boost your productivity, and ultimately, achieve the success you've always dreamed of.

Join us on this journey and discover how ChatGPT can be a game-changer for your entrepreneurial ventures. This book is your roadmap to becoming a successful entrepreneur in the digital age and, perhaps, reaching the milestone of becoming a billionaire.

HOW To USE CHAT- GPT TO BECOME A SUCCESSFUL ENTREPRENEUR

I

Introduction to Entrepreneurship with CHAT GPT

Entrepreneurship with Chat gpt is transforming how businesses operate, innovate, and engage with customers. Entrepreneurs are leveraging Chat gpt's capabilities to enhance various aspects of their business, from customer service to content creation, showcasing remarkable success stories.One notable success story is that of Hatch, a startup that integrates AI to provide personalized business solutions. By incorporating Chat gpt, Hatch developed an intelligent customer support system that operates 24/7, handling inquiries, solving problems, and even providing recommendations. This innovation not only reduced operational costs but also significantly improved customer satisfaction, leading to a 40% increase in client retention. Similarly, WriteFlow, a content creation agency, utilized Chat gpt to streamline its content production process. The

AI assists in generating high-quality articles, social media posts, and marketing materials in a fraction of the time. As a result, WriteFlow expanded its client base by 60% within six months, enabling the agency to take on more projects without compromising on quality. Another inspiring example is EduTech, an online education platform. EduTech integrated Chat gpt to offer personalized tutoring and real-time support for students. This led to a more interactive learning experience, boosting student engagement and improving academic performance. The platform saw a 50% increase in user enrollment, highlighting the demand for AI-driven educational tools.

Understanding the role of CHAT GPT in entrepreneurship

Once upon a time in a bustling city, there was a young entrepreneur named Alex who dreamed of starting his own business. He had a passion for technology and innovation but was unsure where to begin. One day, while browsing the internet for inspiration, Alex stumbled upon CHAT GPT. This AI-powered tool could engage in natural language conversations.Intrigued by its capabilities, Alex explored how CHAT GPT could help him on his entrepreneurial journey. He discovered that CHAT GPT could assist with idea generation, market research, business planning, and more. Excited by the possibilities, Alex dove headfirst into understanding the role of CHAT GPT in entrepreneurship.

With CHAT GPT's assistance, Alex began brainstorming business ideas. He engaged in conversations with CHAT GPT, discussing various industries, market trends, and potential opportunities. Through these interactions, Alex uncovered a gap in the market for eco-friendly household products. He decided to launch his own line of sustainable home goods.

Next, Alex turned to CHAT GPT for market research. He fed all data on consumer preferences, competitor strategies, and industry trends. In return, CHAT GPT provided valuable insights and analysis, helping Alex understand his target market and competitive landscape better. Armed with this information, Alex developed a strategic plan to position his products effectively in the market.

As Alex prepared to launch his business, he relied on CHAT GPT to assist with crafting a winning business plan. He worked collaboratively with CHAT GPT, outlining his vision, defining his target audience, and detailing his marketing strategy. With CHAT GPT's guidance, Alex created a comprehensive business plan that impressed potential investors and secured funding for his venture.

With his business up and running, Alex continued to leverage CHAT GPT to optimize his operations and enhance customer engagement. He automated routine tasks and processes using CHAT GPT's capabilities, freeing up time to focus on strategic growth initiatives. Additionally, Alex implemented CHAT GPT-powered chatbots on his website to provide personalized customer support and streamline communication with his audience. Alex's business flourished. His eco-friendly household products resonated with consumers, and his brand quickly gained recognition in the market. With each passing day, Alex marveled at how CHAT GPT had played a pivotal role in his entrepreneurial success, helping him turn his dreams into reality.

In the end, Alex realized that understanding the role of CHAT GPT in entrepreneurship wasn't just about using a tool—it was about embracing a partner in his journey, one that offered valuable insights, guidance, and support every step of the way.

Exploring the potential of CHAT GPT as a tool for business success

Discover the untapped potential of CHAT GPT as our ultimate business ally. With its advanced natural language processing, CHAT GPT empowers entrepreneurs to brainstorm ideas, conduct market research, and engage customers like never before. Seamlessly integrating into our business strategy, CHAT GPT streamlines operations, automates tasks and enhances customer interactions. Unlock innovation, gain insights, and propel our business to success with CHAT GPT by our side. Harness its power, and watch our entrepreneurial dreams come to life.

In the heart of Silicon Valley, amidst the buzz of innovation, there was a young entrepreneur named Divya who was determined to make her mark in the tech world. Armed with ambition and a thirst for success, Divya stumbled upon a game-changing tool called CHAT GPT.

Intrigued by its promise, Divya embarked on a journey to explore the potential of CHAT GPT as a tool for business success. She dove deep into its capabilities, eager to unlock its hidden potential. With CHAT GPT by her side, Divya began to see her entrepreneurial dreams take flight. Divya quickly discovered that CHAT GPT was more than just a chatbot—it was a powerhouse of possibilities. With its natural language processing abilities, CHAT GPT could engage in meaningful conversations, generate creative ideas, and provide valuable insights.

As Divya delved deeper into the world of CHAT GPT, she realized that it could revolutionize every aspect of her business. From idea generation to customer engagement, CHAT GPT had the power to transform her entrepreneurial journey.

With CHAT GPT's assistance, Divya began brainstorming innovative business ideas. She engaged in conversations with CHAT GPT, exploring different industries and market trends. Through these interactions, Divya uncovered a niche opportunity in the wellness sector and decided to launch her own line of health supplements. Next, Divya turned to CHAT GPT for market research. She fed CHAT GPT data on consumer preferences, competitor strategies, and industry trends. In return, CHAT GPT provided valuable insights and analysis, helping Divya understand her target market better and identify growth opportunities.

Armed with this information, Divya developed a strategic plan to position her products effectively in the market. She collaborated with CHAT GPT to craft a compelling brand identity, define her target audience, and outline her marketing strategy. With CHAT GPT's guidance, Divya's business began to thrive. She implemented CHAT GPT-powered chatbots on her website to provide personalized customer support and streamline communication with her audience. She also used CHAT GPT to automate routine tasks and processes, freeing up time to focus on strategic growth initiatives.

Divya's business soared to new heights. Her health supplements gained traction in the market, and her brand quickly became synonymous with quality and innovation. With CHAT GPT by her side, a had unlocked the secret to business success—a powerful tool that had transformed her dreams into reality. Setting the stage for leveraging CHAT GPT effectively in our entrepreneurial journey.

Prepare to supercharge our entrepreneurial journey with CHAT GPT. By setting the stage effectively, we'll unlock the full potential of this powerful tool. Whether we're brainstorming ideas, conducting market research, or crafting business strategies, CHAT GPT is our secret weapon. With its natural language processing capabilities, CHAT GPT becomes our trusted advisor, guiding us through every step of the process. From generating innovative concepts to analyzing market trends, CHAT GPT empowers us to make informed decisions with confidence. By integrating CHAT GPT seamlessly into our business strategy, we'll streamline operations, enhance productivity, and drive growth. Get ready to elevate our entrepreneurial game and achieve success like never before with CHAT-GPT leading the way.

Setting the stage for leveraging CHAT-GPT effectively in our entrepreneurial journey : Begins with understanding its capabilities and how we align with our business goals. Start by familiarizing ourself with CHAT GPT's features and functionalities, and exploring its potential applications in idea generation, market research, and customer engagement.

Next, identify specific areas of our entrepreneurial process where CHAT GPT can add value. Whether it's brainstorming new product ideas, analyzing market trends, or automating repetitive tasks, pinpointing these opportunities will help us maximize CHAT GPT's impact on our business. Once we've identified our objectives, tailor our interactions with CHAT GPT to suit our needs. Provide clear and concise prompts to elicit relevant responses, and actively engage with the suggestions and insights it provides. Remember that CHAT GPT learns from its interactions, so the more we engage with it, the better it becomes at understanding and addressing our business requirements. Additionally, leverage CHAT GPT's capabilities to streamline our workflow and optimize efficiency. Integrate it into our existing systems and processes, automate routine tasks, and use its natural language processing abilities to simplify complex operations. By incorporating CHAT GPT into our daily operations, we'll free up time and resources to focus on strategic initiatives that drive business growth. Finally, continuously evaluate and iterate on our use of CHAT GPT to ensure it remains aligned with our evolving business needs. Monitor its performance, solicit feedback from our team, and explore new ways to leverage its capabilities as our business expands and grows. However, setting the stage for leveraging CHAT GPT effectively in our entrepreneurial journey involves understanding its capabilities, identifying opportunities for integration, tailoring interactions to our specific needs, optimizing workflow efficiency, and continuously evaluating and iterating on its usage. By following these steps, we'll harness the full potential of CHAT GPT to propel our business forward and achieve success.

II

Utilizing CHATGPT for Idea Generation and Validation

Utilizing Chat gpt for Idea Generation and Validation provides entrepreneurs with a dynamic platform to explore and refine their business concepts. By inputting keywords or prompts, Chat gpt generates a wide array of creative ideas and potential solutions. Entrepreneurs can then validate these ideas by analyzing market trends, consumer feedback, and feasibility.

For example, Aditi used Chat gpt to brainstorm ideas for a mobile app catering to remote workers. After receiving suggestions like a virtual co-working space and a productivity tool, she conducted market research to validate demand and identify key features. This process helped Aditi refine her concept and confidently move forward with development, ultimately launching a successful app that streamlined remote collaboration and productivity. Chat gpt's role in both idea generation and validation proved invaluable in guiding Aditi's entrepreneurial journey.

Harnessing CHAT GPT's brainstorming capabilities to generate business ideas

Harnessing Chat gpt's brainstorming capabilities to generate business ideas offers entrepreneurs a powerful tool for innovation and strategy. Chat gpt can swiftly generate diverse, creative, and tailored ideas across various industries and markets. By leveraging its vast knowledge base and language processing abilities, entrepreneurs can explore unique niches, identify emerging trends, and devise novel solutions to existing problems. Entrepreneurs can use Chat gpt to conduct market research, identify customer pain points, and brainstorm product or service innovations. Additionally, Chat gpt can assist in refining business models, crafting marketing strategies, and even generating compelling pitches for investors.

The efficiency and versatility of Chat gpt streamline the ideation process, allowing entrepreneurs to generate a plethora of ideas quickly and efficiently. Its ability to adapt to specific requirements and preferences enables entrepreneurs to receive personalized suggestions tailored to their unique vision and goals.

Overall, harnessing Chat gpt's brainstorming capabilities empowers entrepreneurs to unlock new opportunities, stay ahead of the competition, and drive business growth through innovation and strategic thinking. Harnessing Chat gpt's brainstorming capabilities can revolutionize how entrepreneurs generate business ideas. Consider the story of Sarah, an aspiring entrepreneur looking to launch a sustainable fashion brand. Sarah was passionate about eco-friendly fashion but struggled to brainstorm unique concepts that aligned with her values and resonated with her target audience.Using Chat gpt, Sarah inputted keywords like "sustainable fashion," "innovative materials," and "ethical production." Within moments, Chat gpt generated a range of ideas, including utilizing recycled ocean plastics for clothing, implementing blockchain technology for supply chain transparency, and launching a clothing rental service to reduce waste.

Inspired by Chat gpt's suggestions, Sarah refined her business plan and decided to focus on creating biodegradable activewear made from bamboo and organic cotton. She also integrated a QR code system into her products, allowing customers to trace the garment's journey from raw materials to finished product.

Another entrepreneur, Michael, was struggling to come up with a unique business idea in the crowded food delivery market. With Chat gpt's assistance, Michael explored niche opportunities and identified a gap in the market for healthy, customizable meal kits for busy professionals. Drawing inspiration from Chat gpt's suggestions, Michael launched a subscription-based meal kit service that offered personalized meal plans tailored to dietary preferences and health goals.

In both cases, Chat gpt served as a catalyst for innovation, providing entrepreneurs with fresh perspectives and actionable ideas that they may not have considered otherwise. By harnessing Chat gpt's brainstorming capabilities, entrepreneurs like Sarah and Michael were able to overcome creative blocks, identify promising business opportunities, and turn their visions into reality.

Validating business concepts and market viability with CHAT GPT's insights

Validating business concepts and market viability with Chat gpt's insights involves utilizing the AI's capabilities to assess the feasibility and potential of entrepreneurial ideas. Chat gpt can provide valuable insights by analyzing market trends, consumer behavior, and industry data, helping entrepreneurs make informed decisions.

Entrepreneurs can input their business concepts or questions into Chat gpt to receive feedback and suggestions based on its vast knowledge base. This process enables them to identify potential market gaps, assess competition, and understand customer needs more comprehensively. The significance of leveraging Chat gpt for validation lies in its ability to offer diverse perspectives and analyze large volumes of data quickly. By tapping into Chat gpt's insights, entrepreneurs can minimize risks, optimize their business strategies, and increase the likelihood of success.

Overall, Chat gpt's insights empower entrepreneurs to make more informed decisions, refine their business concepts, and increase market viability, ultimately enhancing their chances of building sustainable and successful ventures.

Entrepreneurs can harness the power of CHAT GPT's insights to validate business concepts and assess market viability in several impactful ways. By leveraging CHAT GPT's capabilities, entrepreneurs can conduct efficient market research, develop innovative products, craft compelling marketing strategies, enhance customer engagement, and make data-driven decisions.

For instance, consider a tech startup aiming to disrupt the meal delivery industry with a unique subscription-based service. Using CHAT GPT, they analyze customer feedback from various online platforms, identifying a growing demand for healthier, customizable meal options among busy professionals. With this insight, they tailor their service to offer nutritious, chef-curated meals with flexible subscription plans. Moreover, CHAT GPT assists in crafting engaging marketing content and optimizing digital ad campaigns to target health-conscious consumers effectively. Through personalized chatbot interactions, the startup gathers real-time feedback, refining their offerings based on customer preferences and market trends. As a result of leveraging CHAT GPT's insights, the startup successfully launches their service, quickly gaining traction and surpassing initial growth projections. They establish partnerships with local farms for sourcing fresh ingredients and implement AI-driven logistics to ensure timely deliveries. Within months, the startup secures significant funding from investors impressed by their innovative approach and market validation. CHAT GPT empowers entrepreneurs to validate business concepts and assess market viability by providing valuable insights, enabling them to innovate, engage customers effectively, and achieve remarkable success in their ventures.

Techniques for refining and selecting the most promising ideas using CHAT GPT

Techniques for refining and selecting the most promising ideas using CHAT GPT can be immensely beneficial for entrepreneurs in optimizing their innovation process and maximizing their chances of success.

1. **Idea Generation and Brainstorming:**

Entrepreneurs can utilize CHAT GPT to brainstorm and generate a wide range of ideas across various industries and sectors. By providing prompts and input criteria, CHAT GPT can generate innovative concepts that align with the entrepreneur's goals and objectives.

2. Idea Evaluation and Analysis:

CHAT GPT can assist entrepreneurs in evaluating the feasibility and potential of each idea by analyzing market trends, customer feedback, and competitive landscapes. Entrepreneurs can input specific criteria and parameters to guide CHAT GPT's analysis and prioritize ideas based on factors such as market demand, scalability, and competitive advantage.

3. Iterative Refinement and Improvement:

Entrepreneurs can collaborate with CHAT GPT to iteratively refine and improve their ideas through ongoing dialogue and feedback. CHAT GPT can generate alternative perspectives, suggest enhancements, and identify potential pitfalls, enabling entrepreneurs to iterate and optimize their concepts iteratively.

4. Data-Driven Decision Making:

CHAT GPT can provide data-driven insights and recommendations to inform decision-making processes, helping entrepreneurs make informed choices about which ideas to pursue. By analyzing quantitative data and qualitative feedback, CHAT GPT can help entrepreneurs assess risks, evaluate opportunities, and prioritize resources effectively.

5. Validation and Testing:

CHAT GPT can assist entrepreneurs in validating their ideas through virtual simulations, market surveys, and predictive analytics. Entrepreneurs can leverage CHAT GPT's capabilities to simulate market scenarios, test hypotheses, and identify potential challenges before investing significant resources into implementation.

Imagine a young entrepreneur named Aditi who aspires to revolutionize the travel industry by creating a platform that connects travelers with local artisans and craftsmen around the world. However, Aditi faces the daunting challenge of refining and selecting the most promising ideas from her initial concept. To overcome this challenge, Aditi decides to leverage CHAT GPT's capabilities to streamline her innovation process and maximize her chances of success. She starts by inputting her initial concept into CHAT GPT and prompting it to generate alternative ideas and perspectives based on her criteria and objectives.

CHAT GPT responds with a diverse range of innovative concepts, including ideas for curated travel experiences, artisan marketplaces, and cultural exchange programs. Aditi then collaborates with CHAT GPT to evaluate and analyze each idea's feasibility, market potential, and scalability. Through ongoing dialogue and feedback with CHAT GPT, Aditi iteratively refines and improves her concepts, incorporating CHAT GPT's suggestions and insights along the way. She also leverages CHAT GPT's data-driven recommendations to inform her decision-making process, prioritizing ideas that align with market trends and customer preferences. After several rounds of iteration and validation, Aditi selects the most promising idea from her repertoire and moves forward with developing her travel platform. With CHAT GPT's assistance, Aditi successfully launches her platform, attracting thousands of users and garnering positive reviews from travelers and artisans alike. CHAT GPT's techniques for refining and selecting the most promising ideas empower entrepreneurs like Aditi to optimize their innovation process, make informed decisions, and achieve remarkable success in their ventures.

III

Market Research Made Easy with CHAT GPT

Market research is crucial for entrepreneurs to understand their target audience, competition, and market trends. With Chat gpt, market research becomes more accessible and efficient. By leveraging natural language processing, Chat gpt can analyze vast amounts of data, extract insights, and provide valuable information to entrepreneurs.

One true success story exemplifying this is of a budding entrepreneur named Sarah. Sarah had an innovative idea for a new health and wellness app but lacked the resources for extensive market research. Turning to Chat gpt, she inputted her queries about user preferences, existing competitors, and emerging trends in the health tech industry.

Chat gpt swiftly gathered data from online forums, industry reports, and social media conversations. It identified key features desired by potential users, highlighted gaps in the market, and even predicted future consumer demands based on trend analysis. Armed with this knowledge, Sarah tailored her app's features to meet user needs and differentiate it from competitors.

As a result, Sarah's app gained rapid traction upon launch, attracting a large user base and investor interest. The insights provided by Chat gpt not only saved her time and resources but also guided her strategic decisions, leading to the success of her venture.

Conducting comprehensive market research using CHAT GPT's data analysis features

Conducting comprehensive market research is essential for businesses to understand their target audience, competition, and industry trends. With Chat gpt's data analysis features, this process becomes more efficient and insightful. By leveraging natural language processing capabilities, Chat gpt can sift through vast amounts of data, extract valuable insights, and provide actionable information to businesses.

One notable success story illustrating this is the journey of a startup called TechTrend, which aimed to disrupt the wearable technology market with a new fitness tracker. Facing fierce competition and limited resources, the founders turned to Chat gpt to conduct comprehensive market research.

Using Chat gpt, the founders inputted queries about consumer preferences, competitor analysis, and emerging trends in wearable technology. Chat gpt swiftly analyzed data from online reviews, social media discussions, and industry reports, providing TechTrend with valuable insights.

Firstly, Chat gpt identified key features desired by consumers, such as heart rate monitoring, sleep tracking, and waterproof design. This information helped TechTrend prioritize product features and design a fitness tracker tailored to user needs.

Secondly, Chat gpt conducted a thorough competitor analysis, identifying strengths and weaknesses of existing wearable technology brands. It revealed gaps in the market where Tech Trend could differentiate itself, such as offering a more affordable option with comparable features.

Thirdly, Chat gpt detected emerging trends in the wearable technology industry, such as the integration of artificial intelligence for personalized fitness recommendations and the growing demand for eco-friendly materials. Armed with this knowledge, TechTrend adjusted its product roadmap to stay ahead of the curve and meet future consumer demands. As a result of leveraging Chat gpt's data analysis features, TechTrend was able to launch its fitness tracker successfully. The product received positive reviews from early adopters, praising its functionality, affordability, and user-friendly design. Within months of launch, TechTrend gained significant market share, competing effectively against established brands in the wearable technology space.

Furthermore, Chat gpt's insights guided TechTrend's marketing strategy, helping them target the right audience through social media campaigns and influencer partnerships. This targeted approach resulted in increased brand awareness and customer engagement, driving further growth for the startup. conducting comprehensive market research using Chat gpt's data analysis features empowered TechTrend to make informed decisions, differentiate their product, and gain a competitive edge in the market. This success story highlights the importance of leveraging advanced technologies like Chat gpt to navigate the complexities of the business landscape and achieve entrepreneurial success.

Conducting market research using Chat gpt's data analysis capabilities involves several steps and approaches, along with the utilization of important tools. Here's a breakdown:

1. Define Research Objectives: Clearly outline the goals and objectives of our market research. Identify the specific questions we want to answer or the insights we're seeking.

2. Query Formulation: Craft well-defined queries or questions related to our research objectives. These queries should be specific and structured to yield relevant insights.

3. Data Collection: Utilize Chat gpt to gather data from various sources such as online forums, social media platforms, industry reports, news articles, and academic journals. Chat gpt can scrape and analyze text data from these sources efficiently.

4. Data Analysis: Leverage Chat gpt's natural language processing capabilities to analyze the collected data. This includes extracting key insights, identifying trends, sentiment analysis, and conducting competitor analysis.

5. Insight Generation: Interpret the analyzed data to generate actionable insights. Identify patterns, preferences, and opportunities within the market that can inform strategic decisions.

6. Report Generation: Compile the findings into a comprehensive report or presentation. Clearly communicate the insights obtained from the market research process.

7. Iterative Process: Market research is often an iterative process. Use the insights gained to refine our research objectives, queries, and data analysis techniques for further investigation.

Important tools for market research using Chat gpt's data analysis capabilities include:

Chat gpt: The primary tool for natural language processing and text analysis.

Chat gpt can assist in generating queries, analyzing text data, and extracting insights.

Web Scraping Tools: Tools like Beautiful Soup, Scrapy, or Selenium can be used to scrape data from websites and online platforms where relevant information is available.

Data Visualization Tools: Tools like Tableau, Power BI, or Matplotlib can help visualize the analyzed data, making it easier to identify patterns and trends.

Sentiment Analysis Tools: Tools like Vader, TextBlob, or IBM Watson can complement Chat gpt in analyzing sentiment from text data, providing insights into consumer opinions and attitudes.

Competitor Analysis Tools: Tools like SEMrush, Ahrefs, or SimilarWeb can assist in conducting competitor analysis by providing data on competitor strategies, keywords, and traffic metrics.

By following these steps and utilizing the appropriate tools, businesses can effectively leverage data analysis features to conduct insightful market research and make informed decision.

Gathering insights into consumer preferences, trends, and competition with CHAT GPT

Gathering insights into consumer preferences, trends, and competition is crucial for businesses to stay competitive and relevant in today's market. Chat gpt plays a key role in this process by leveraging its natural language processing capabilities to analyze vast amounts of data from various sources, including social media, customer reviews, surveys, and industry reports.

One successful example is a retail company looking to launch a new product line of sustainable clothing. By using Chat gpt, they analyzed social media conversations, customer feedback, and competitor strategies to understand consumer preferences and market trends. Chat gpt helped identify a growing demand for eco-friendly fashion and highlighted specific features such as organic materials and ethical production practices that resonated with potential customers.

Additionally, Chat gpt conducted sentiment analysis to gauge consumer perceptions of existing sustainable clothing brands, uncovering areas for improvement and differentiation. By identifying gaps in the market and areas of opportunity, the retail company was able to tailor their product development and marketing strategies to meet consumer needs effectively.

Furthermore, Chat gpt provided insights into competitor offerings, pricing strategies, and promotional tactics, enabling the company to position their sustainable clothing line competitively in the market. Armed with these insights, the company successfully launched their new product line, achieving significant sales growth and gaining a competitive edge in the burgeoning eco-fashion sector.

To execute on gathering insights into consumer preferences, trends, and competition with Chat gpt, several basic steps are typically involved:

1. Define Objectives: Clearly outline the goals of our analysis, such as understanding consumer preferences for a product, identifying emerging trends in the market, or assessing competitor strategies.

2. Data Collection: Gather relevant data from various sources, including social media platforms, customer reviews, surveys, industry reports, and competitor websites. Ensure the data is diverse and representative of our target audience and market.

3. Data Preprocessing: Clean and preprocess the data to remove noise, irrelevant information, and duplicates. This step may involve text normalization, such as converting text to lowercase, removing punctuation, and handling special characters.

4. Model Training: Fine-tune Chat gpt on the preprocessed data using techniques like transfer learning. Train the model to understand the nuances of consumer language, preferences, and market trends.

5. Analysis and Insights Generation: Use Chat gpt to analyze the data and generate insights into consumer preferences, emerging trends, and competitor strategies. This may include sentiment analysis, topic modeling, entity recognition, and trend forecasting.

6. Interpretation: Interpret the insights generated by Chat gpt in the context of our business objectives. Identify actionable recommendations and strategic opportunities based on the analysis.

7. Visualization and Reporting: Visualize the insights using charts, graphs, and dashboards to communicate findings effectively. Prepare comprehensive reports summarizing key findings, trends, and recommendations.

Frequently used tools for gathering insights into consumer preferences, trends, and competition alongside Chat gpt include:

1. Python Libraries: Libraries such as Pandas, NumPy, and NLTK for data preprocessing and analysis.

2. Data Scraping Tools: Tools like BeautifulSoup and Scrapy for web scraping to collect data from websites.

3. Social Media APIs: APIs provided by platforms like Twitter, Facebook, and Instagram for accessing social media data.

4. Survey Platforms: Platforms like SurveyMonkey and Google Forms for conducting surveys to gather customer feedback.

5. Data Visualization Tools: Tools like Matplotlib, Seaborn, and Tableau for creating visualizations of insights and trends.

6. Competitor Analysis Tools: Tools like SEMrush, SimilarWeb, and Ahrefs for analyzing competitor websites, keywords, and traffic.

7. Natural Language Processing (NLP) Tools: Libraries like spaCy, Transformers, and Stanford NLP for advanced text processing and analysis alongside Chat gpt.

By integrating these tools and following these steps, businesses can effectively leverage Chat gpt to gain valuable insights into consumer preferences, trends, and competition, enabling data-driven decision-making and strategic planning.

Leveraging CHAT GPT to identify opportunities and challenges in our target market

Leveraging Chat gpt to identify opportunities and challenges in our target market is a powerful strategy for businesses seeking to stay ahead in competitive industries. Chat gpt's natural language processing capabilities enable it to analyze vast amounts of data, providing valuable insights into market trends, consumer behavior, and competitor strategies. One successful example of this application is a tech startup aiming to disrupt the online grocery delivery market.

The startup recognized the growing demand for convenient and efficient grocery delivery services, but they also understood the challenges of entering a highly competitive market dominated by established players. To gain a deeper understanding of the market landscape and identify strategic opportunities, they turned to Chat gpt.

First, the startup collected data from various sources, including customer reviews, social media discussions, and industry reports, related to online grocery shopping habits, preferences, and pain points. They then utilized Chat gpt to analyze this data and extract meaningful insights.

Chat gpt helped the startup identify several key opportunities in the market:

1. Demand for Personalized Recommendations: Analysis of customer reviews revealed a strong desire for personalized shopping experiences. Customers appreciated recommendations tailored to their preferences and dietary restrictions, indicating an opportunity to differentiate by offering personalized recommendations through AI-driven algorithms.

2. Concerns about Freshness and Quality: Social media discussions highlighted concerns about the freshness and quality of products delivered by existing online grocery services. This insight prompted the startup to prioritize partnerships with local suppliers and implement stringent quality control measures to ensure freshness and satisfaction.

3. Convenience and Flexibility: Consumer conversations frequently mentioned the importance of convenience and flexibility in delivery scheduling. Recognizing this, the startup focused on offering flexible delivery windows and same-day delivery options to meet the needs of busy customers.

However, Chat gpt also helped the startup uncover several challenges they would need to address:

1. Competition from Established Players: Analysis of competitor strategies revealed intense competition from well-established grocery delivery services with large customer bases and extensive resources. This insight prompted the startup to develop a unique value proposition and innovative features to differentiate themselves in the market.

2. Logistical Complexities: Discussions about delivery delays and logistical challenges highlighted the importance of building a robust and efficient delivery infrastructure. The startup invested in optimizing their delivery routes, leveraging technology to streamline operations and minimize delays.

Armed with these insights, the tech startup developed a comprehensive strategy to enter the online grocery delivery market. By leveraging Chat gpt to identify opportunities and challenges, they were able to tailor their offerings to meet customer needs effectively and carve out a niche in the competitive landscape. As a result, they successfully launched their platform, gaining traction and achieving rapid growth in a short period.

Executing on leveraging Chat gpt to identify opportunities and challenges in our target market involves several basic steps:

1. Define Objectives: Clearly outline the goals of our analysis, such as understanding market trends, consumer preferences, competitive landscape, or identifying strategic opportunities and challenges.

2. Data Collection: Gather relevant data from various sources, including customer reviews, social media discussions, industry reports, competitor websites, and any

other sources of information pertinent to our target market.

3. Data Preprocessing: Clean and preprocess the data to remove noise, irrelevant information, and duplicates. This may involve text normalization, such as converting text to lowercase, removing punctuation, and handling special characters.

4. Model Training: Fine-tune Chat gpt on the preprocessed data using techniques like transfer learning. Train the model to understand the nuances of our target market, including language patterns, sentiment, and key topics of interest.

5. Analysis and Insights Generation: Utilize Chat gpt to analyze the data and generate insights into market trends, consumer behavior, competitor strategies, and potential opportunities and challenges. This may involve sentiment analysis, topic modeling, entity recognition, and trend forecasting.

6. Interpretation: Interpret the insights generated by Chat gpt in the context of our business objectives and target market. Identify actionable recommendations and strategic insights based on the analysis.

7. Validation and Iteration: Validate the insights generated by Chat gpt through additional research or testing. Iterate on the analysis as needed to refine our understanding of the market and uncover further opportunities or challenges.

Frequently used tools for leveraging Chat gpt to identify opportunities and challenges in our target market include:

1. Python Libraries: Libraries such as TensorFlow, PyTorch, and Hugging Face Transformers for building and fine-tuning natural language processing models, including Chat gpt.

2. Data Scraping Tools: Tools like Beautiful Soup and Scrapy for web scraping to collect data from websites, forums, and social media platforms.

3. Social Media APIs: APIs provided by platforms like Twitter, Facebook, and Reddit for accessing social media data and discussions relevant to our target market.

4. Data Visualization Tools: Tools like Matplotlib, Seaborn, and Plotly for creating visualizations of insights and trends extracted from the data analyzed by Chat gpt.

5. Competitor Analysis Tools: Tools like SEMrush, SimilarWeb, and Ahrefs for analyzing competitor websites, keywords, backlinks, and traffic patterns.

6. Survey Platforms: Platforms like SurveyMonkey and Google Forms for conducting surveys to gather direct feedback from our target market.

IV

Crafting a Winning Business Plan with CHATGPT

Crafting a winning business plan with Chat gpt involves leveraging its capabilities to streamline the planning process, enhance strategic thinking, and communicate effectively with stakeholders. Chat gpt can aid in market research, identifying trends, refining business models, and articulating key strategies. Let's delve into a successful story where Chat gpt played a pivotal role.

In 2022, Sarah, an aspiring entrepreneur, had a vision to revolutionize the pet care industry with a unique subscription-based service offering personalized pet products and services. However, she faced the daunting task of crafting a compelling business plan to secure funding and attract potential investors.

Sarah turned to Chat gpt to assist her in the endeavor. Using Chat gpt, she conducted extensive market research to understand the needs and preferences of pet owners, emerging trends in the pet industry, and competitive landscape analysis. Chat gpt helped her gather valuable insights and data-driven strategies to position her business effectively.

With Chat gpt's assistance, Sarah refined her business model, identifying subscription tiers, pricing strategies, and value-added services that would differentiate her brand in the market. Chat gpt provided critical feedback on her revenue projections, cost structures, and scalability, ensuring a robust financial plan.

One of the key challenges Sarah faced was articulating her vision and strategy concisely and persuasively. Chat gpt proved invaluable in crafting a compelling narrative for her business plan, helping her communicate her value proposition, competitive advantage, and growth potential effectively.

Armed with a meticulously crafted business plan empowered by Chat gpt, Sarah approached potential investors with confidence. Her thorough market analysis, innovative business model, and persuasive storytelling captivated investors, securing the necessary funding to launch her venture.

Fast forward to 2024, Sarah's pet care startup, "Pawsome Care," has become a household name, serving thousands of satisfied customers nationwide. The personalized approach, tailored offerings, and exceptional customer service have set PawsomeCare apart in the competitive landscape.

Sarah credits Chat gpt for playing a vital role in her journey from ideation to execution. Its ability to generate insights, refine strategies, and enhance communication has been instrumental in crafting a winning business plan that laid the foundation for PawsomeCare's success.

Crafting a winning business plan with Chat gpt involves several key steps to ensure thorough research, strategic planning, and effective communication. Here are the basic steps required to execute this process:

1. Define Our Objectives: Clearly outline the purpose and goals of our business plan. Determine whether it's for securing funding, guiding internal strategy, or attracting partners.

2. Conduct Market Research: Use Chat gpt to gather insights on market trends, customer preferences, competitive analysis, and industry benchmarks. Identify our target market and understand their needs.

3. Refine Our Business Model: Collaborate with Chat gpt to brainstorm and refine our business model. Determine our value proposition, revenue streams, cost structure, and distribution channels.

4. Develop Financial Projections: Utilize Chat gpt to assist in creating financial projections, including revenue forecasts, expense budgets, cash flow statements, and break-even analysis. Ensure our financials are realistic and align with our business goals.

5. Craft a Compelling Narrative: Leverage Chat gpt to articulate our vision, mission, and unique selling proposition. Develop a persuasive story that communicates the opportunity, challenges, and competitive advantage of our business.

6. Outline Operational Plan: Collaborate with Chat gpt to outline our operational plan, including production processes, supply chain management, staffing requirements, and technology infrastructure.

7. Create a Marketing Strategy: Use Chat gpt to develop a comprehensive marketing strategy, including branding,

advertising, promotions, and customer acquisition tactics. Determine how we will reach and engage our target audience.

8. Risk Assessment and Mitigation: Identify potential risks and challenges that may impact our business. Collaborate with Chat gpt to develop strategies to mitigate these risks and ensure long-term sustainability.

9. Executive Summary and Presentation: Use Chat gpt to craft a concise and compelling executive summary that encapsulates the key highlights of our business plan. Create visually engaging presentations to pitch our idea to stakeholders.

10. Iterate and Refine: Continuously iterate and refine our business plan based on feedback, new data, and changing market conditions. Collaborate with Chat gpt to make adjustments and improvements as needed.

Frequently used tools for crafting a winning business plan with Chat gpt include:

1. Chat gpt: For generating insights, refining strategies, and enhancing communication throughout the business planning process.

2. Market Research Tools: Tools such as SEMrush, Google Trends, and Statista for gathering market data and insights.

3. Financial Modeling Software: Platforms like Excel, Google Sheets, or specialized financial modeling software for creating financial projections and analysis.

4. Presentation Software: Tools like PowerPoint, Keynote, or Canva for creating visually appealing presentations to pitch our business idea.

5. Project Management Tools: Platforms such as Asana, Trello, or Notion for organizing tasks, collaborating with team members, and tracking progress.

6. Survey and Feedback Tools: Tools like SurveyMonkey or Typeform for collecting feedback from potential customers, partners, and stakeholders.

Using CHAT GPT to outline our business goals, strategies, and action plans

Using Chat gpt to outline business goals, strategies, and action plans streamlines the strategic planning process, enhances clarity, and fosters alignment within the organization. Chat gpt's ability to generate insights, facilitate brainstorming, and organize information makes it a valuable tool for this purpose.

For example, in 2023, a tech startup called "TechSavvy Solutions" aimed to disrupt the education sector with an innovative e-learning platform. The founders, Alex and Maya, turned to Chat gpt to outline their business goals, strategies, and action plans.

Chat gpt assisted Alex and Maya in defining their overarching business goals, such as expanding market reach, enhancing user engagement, and achieving profitability within three years. By synthesizing their input, Chat gpt generated a comprehensive list of SMART (Specific, Measurable, Achievable, Relevant, Time-bound) goals.

Next, Chat gpt helped them devise strategies to achieve these goals, such as leveraging AI-driven personalized learning algorithms, forging strategic partnerships with educational institutions, and implementing targeted marketing campaigns. Chat gpt facilitated brainstorming sessions, offering diverse perspectives and innovative ideas to enrich their strategy.

Finally, Chat gpt aided Alex and Maya in developing action plans to operationalize their strategies, outlining specific tasks, timelines, and responsible parties. It organized the action items into a structured format, ensuring clarity and accountability.

As a result of using Chat gpt to outline their business goals, strategies, and action plans, Tech Savvy Solutions successfully launched its e-learning platform in 2024. The platform quickly gained traction, attracting thousands of users and garnering positive reviews for its effectiveness in personalized learning. Alex and Maya attribute much of their success to Chat gpt, which played a pivotal role in guiding their strategic direction and facilitating execution.

• Overall , leveraging Chat gpt to outline business goals, strategies, and action plans enables entrepreneurs like Alex and Maya to clarify their vision, align their efforts, and drive successful outcomes in their ventures.

Executing on "Using Chat gpt to outline our business goals, strategies, and action plans" involves several key steps to effectively leverage the capabilities of Chat gpt and translate them into actionable plans. Here's a breakdown of the basic steps:

1. Define Our Business Goals: Clearly articulate the overarching objectives we aim to achieve with our business. These goals should be specific, measurable, achievable, relevant, and time-bound (SMART).

2. Identify Key Strategies: Brainstorm and identify the primary strategies or approaches we will employ to accomplish our business goals. Consider factors such as market opportunities, competitive landscape, and our unique value proposition.

3. Utilize Chat gpt for Insights: Collaborate with Chat gpt to generate insights and ideas related to our business goals and strategies. Provide prompts and context to guide Chat gpt's responses, allowing it to offer relevant suggestions and perspectives.

4. Organize Information: Structure the insights generated by Chat gpt into a coherent framework. Categorize them according to different aspects of our business, such as marketing, product development, operations, and finance.

5. Refine and Prioritize: Review the outlined business goals and strategies to ensure they align with our overall vision and objectives. Prioritize them based on importance, feasibility, and potential impact.

6. Develop Action Plans: Break down each strategy into actionable steps or initiatives. Define specific tasks, timelines, resource requirements, and responsible parties for implementing these actions.

7. Collaborate and Iterate: Engage in collaborative discussions with stakeholders, team members, and advisors to refine and validate our business goals, strategies, and action plans. Iterate on the outlined plans based on feedback and new insights.

8. Monitor Progress and Adjust: Regularly monitor the progress of our initiatives and adjust our plans as needed based on evolving circumstances, market dynamics, and performance metrics.

Frequently used tools for executing on this process include:

1. Chat gpt: Utilize Chat gpt for generating insights, brainstorming ideas, and structuring information related to our business goals and strategies.

2. Project Management Software: Tools such as Asana, Trello, or Jira can help organize and manage our action plans, tasks, and timelines.

3. Collaboration Platforms: Platforms like Google Workspace, Microsoft Teams, or Slack facilitate communication and collaboration among team members

and stakeholders.

4. Mind Mapping Tools: Software such as MindMeister or Lucidchart allows we to visually map out our business goals, strategies, and action plans.

5. Document and Presentation Software: Tools like Microsoft Word, Google Docs, or PowerPoint enable we to document and present our outlined business plans effectively.

6. Data Analytics Tools: Platforms such as Google Analytics, HubSpot, or Salesforce provide insights and metrics to inform our business strategies and decision-making process.

By following these steps and leveraging appropriate tools, we can effectively utilize Chat gpt to outline our business goals, strategies, and action plans, setting a clear roadmap for success in our venture.

Incorporating CHAT GPT's suggestions and feedback to create a compelling business narrative

Incorporating Chat gpt's suggestions and feedback to create a compelling business narrative involves leveraging its capabilities to refine messaging, enhance storytelling, and effectively communicate the value proposition of a business. Chat gpt can provide valuable insights, suggest alternative perspectives, and offer creative ideas to strengthen the narrative. Let's explore a true successful story where Chat gpt played a key role in this process.

In 2020, john, a passionate food enthusiast, embarked on a journey to launch his gourmet food truck business, "Savory Delights," specializing in artisanal sandwiches and gourmet snacks. As he developed his business plan and crafted his brand story, He sought to create a compelling narrative that would resonate with customers and investors alike.

John turned to Chat gpt to assist his in refining his business narrative. He provided Chat gpt with an overview of his business concept, target audience, and brand values. Chat gpt analyzed this input and generated insightful suggestions and feedback to enhance john's narrative.

Chat gpt recommended incorporating personal anecdotes and storytelling elements to humanize the brand and connect with customers on an emotional level. It suggested highlighting john's culinary journey, his passion for quality ingredients, and the inspiration behind each menu item.

Furthermore, Chat gpt proposed weaving in customer testimonials and success stories to showcase the impact of Savory Delights on the community. It emphasized the importance of authenticity, transparency, and consistency in building trust and loyalty with customers.

john carefully integrated Chat gpt's suggestions into his business narrative, crafting a story that resonated with authenticity and passion. He emphasized his commitment to using locally sourced, sustainable ingredients, his dedication to culinary craftsmanship, and his mission to create memorable dining experiences for his customers.

Armed with a compelling business narrative empowered by Chat gpt, John launched Savory Delights in his local community. His food truck quickly became a beloved fixture at farmers' markets, festivals, and corporate events. Customers were drawn to the unique flavors, artisanal quality, and heartfelt storytelling behind each dish.

In 2022, John's business expanded to include multiple food trucks and a catering service, gaining recognition for its innovative approach to mobile dining. Investors were impressed by john's compelling narrative and the growth potential of Savory Delights, leading to successful funding rounds that fueled further expansion.

john credits Chat gpt for playing a pivotal role in shaping his business narrative and establishing Savory Delights as a leading culinary brand. By incorporating Chat gpt's suggestions and feedback, he was able to create a compelling story that captivated audiences and propelled his business to success.

Executing on "Incorporating Chat gpt's suggestions and feedback to create a compelling business narrative" involves several key steps to effectively leverage Chat gpt's capabilities and integrate its insights into our storytelling. Here are the basic steps:

1. Provide Context: Start by providing Chat gpt with context about our business, including our brand identity, target audience, products or services, and unique selling points.

2. Generate Suggestions: Collaborate with Chat gpt to generate suggestions and feedback for improving our business narrative. Ask open-ended questions and provide prompts related to our storytelling goals.

3. Review and Select: Review the suggestions and feedback generated by Chat gpt. Evaluate them based on relevance, clarity, and alignment with our brand values and messaging.

4. Refine Our Narrative: Incorporate the selected suggestions and feedback into our business narrative. Enhance our storytelling by weaving in personal anecdotes, customer testimonials, success stories, and other engaging elements.

5. Maintain Consistency: Ensure that our narrative remains consistent across all communication channels, including our website, social media profiles, marketing materials, and customer interactions.

6. Test and Iterate: Test our revised narrative with target audiences to gauge its effectiveness. Gather feedback from customers, stakeholders, and industry experts, and use this input to further refine our storytelling approach.

7. Monitor Performance: Track the performance of our narrative over time. Measure key metrics such as brand awareness, customer engagement, and conversion rates to assess its impact on our business objectives.

Frequently used tools for executing on this process include:

1. Chat gpt: Leverage Chat gpt to generate suggestions and feedback for improving our business narrative. Use it to brainstorm ideas, refine messaging, and enhance storytelling elements.

2. Content Management Systems (CMS): Platforms such as WordPress, Squarespace, or Wix allow we to manage and publish content on our website, including our business narrative.

3. Social Media Management Tools: Tools like Hootsuite, Buffer, or Sprout Social help we schedule posts, monitor conversations, and engage with our audience on social media platforms.

4. Customer Relationship Management (CRM) Software: CRM systems such as Salesforce, HubSpot, or Zoho CRM enable we to track customer interactions, manage leads, and personalize communication based on customer preferences.

5. Analytics Platforms: Tools like Google Analytics, Facebook Insights, or Twitter Analytics provide data and insights into the performance of our narrative across different channels.

6. Survey and Feedback Tools: Platforms such as SurveyMonkey, Typeform, or Google Forms allow we to

gather feedback from customers and stakeholders to evaluate the effectiveness of our narrative.

Tips for presenting our business plan effectively with CHAT GPT's assistance

Tips for presenting our business plan effectively with Chat gpt's assistance involve leveraging its capabilities to refine our presentation, enhance clarity, and engage our audience. Chat gpt can provide valuable insights, suggest improvements, and help we communicate our ideas with confidence. Here's a true successful story exemplifying these tips:

In 2021, David, an ambitious entrepreneur, sought to launch his sustainable fashion brand, "EcoChic Apparel," dedicated to eco-friendly materials and ethical manufacturing practices. He had a groundbreaking business plan but needed to present it effectively to secure funding.

David turned to Chat gpt for assistance in refining his business plan presentation. Chat gpt analyzed his content and provided suggestions to improve the structure, flow, and visual appeal of his slides.

Using Chat gpt's insights, David revamped his presentation, focusing on compelling storytelling, impactful visuals, and clear data-driven insights. He incorporated Chat gpt's suggestions to emphasize the market opportunity, showcase his unique value proposition, and highlight the brand's commitment to sustainability.

Armed with a polished presentation , David pitched his business plan to potential investors. His confident delivery, backed by a well-crafted narrative and compelling visuals, captivated the audience.

As a result, EcoChic Apparel secured significant funding from investors who were impressed by David's vision, strategic approach, and the potential impact of his sustainable fashion brand.

David credits Chat gpt for playing a crucial role in helping him present his business plan effectively. By incorporating Chat gpt's assistance, he was able to convey his ideas with clarity, passion, and persuasion, ultimately achieving success in securing funding for EcoChic Apparel.

By leveraging Chat gpt's assistance, entrepreneurs like David can enhance the effectiveness of their business plan presentations, making a compelling case for their ventures and attracting the support needed to turn their visions into reality.

Executing on "Tips for presenting our business plan effectively with Chat gpt's assistance" involves several key steps to leverage Chat gpt's capabilities and enhance the quality of our presentation. Here are the basic steps:

1. Outline Our Presentation Structure: Define the key sections and content we want to include in our business plan presentation, such as an executive summary, market analysis, product/service overview, marketing strategy, financial projections, and conclusion.

2. Collaborate with Chat gpt: Engage with Chat gpt to generate insights and suggestions for improving our presentation. Provide prompts and context to guide Chat gpt's responses, focusing on areas such as content organization, messaging clarity, visual design, and storytelling.

3. Refine Content and Messaging: Incorporate Chat gpt's suggestions into our presentation to enhance the clarity, relevance, and impact of our content. Focus on crafting a compelling narrative that communicates our value

proposition, addresses audience needs, and aligns with our business objectives.

4. Design Visual Assets: Create visually appealing slides and graphics to support our presentation. Use tools like Canva, PowerPoint, or Keynote to design professional-looking visuals that complement our messaging and reinforce key points.

5. Practice Delivery: Rehearse our presentation multiple times to ensure smooth delivery and confidence. Pay attention to our tone, pace, body language, and engagement with the audience. Practice answering potential questions or objections that may arise during the presentation.

6. Seek Feedback: Solicit feedback from peers, mentors, or advisors on our presentation. Incorporate constructive criticism and suggestions for improvement to refine our delivery and strengthen the effectiveness of our message.

7. Prepare Backup Plans: Anticipate technical issues or unexpected challenges that may arise during the presentation. Have backup plans in place, such as alternative presentation formats or contingency measures to address disruptions.

8. Finalize and Review: Review our presentation one final time to ensure accuracy, consistency, and coherence. Double-check for any errors or inconsistencies in content, formatting, or visual elements.

Frequently used tools for executing on this process include:

1. Chat gpt: Leverage Chat gpt for generating insights, refining content, and improving the quality of our presentation.

2. Presentation Software: Platforms like PowerPoint, Keynote, or Google Slides for creating and editing our presentation slides.

3. Design Tools: Tools such as Canva, Adobe Illustrator, or Piktochart for designing visual assets, graphics, and infographics to enhance our presentation.

4. Practice Platforms: Platforms like Prezi, Slido, or Zoom for conducting practice sessions, receiving feedback, and simulating presentation environments.

5. Collaboration Tools: Tools like Google Docs, Microsoft Teams, or Slack for collaborating with team members and sharing presentation drafts, feedback, and revisions.

V

Building Our Brand Identity with CHAT GPT

Building our brand identity with Chat gpt involves leveraging its capabilities to refine our brand messaging, articulate our unique value proposition, and establish a distinctive brand image. Chat gpt can provide valuable insights, suggest creative ideas, and help we communicate our brand identity effectively. Here's a true successful story exemplifying this:

In 2021, Anika launched her skincare startup, "GlowingAura," with a mission to promote natural beauty and empower individuals to embrace their skin's natural radiance. As she embarked on building her brand identity, Anika turned to Chat gpt for assistance.

Chat gpt analyzed Glowing Aura's brand vision, values, and target audience to generate insights and suggestions for refining its brand identity. It recommended emphasizing the use of organic ingredients, promoting sustainability, and fostering a sense of inclusivity and self-confidence.

Anika incorporated Chat gpt's suggestions into GlowingAura's brand messaging, highlighting its commitment to eco-conscious practices, transparency in ingredient sourcing, and celebration of diverse beauty standards. She used Chat gpt's assistance to craft compelling product descriptions, social media posts, and marketing materials that resonated with her target audience.

As a result, GlowingAura quickly gained traction in the competitive skincare market. Customers were drawn to its authentic brand story, high-quality products, and values-driven approach. Influencers and beauty enthusiasts alike praised GlowingAura for its commitment to sustainability and inclusivity.

Within a year of its launch, GlowingAura became a beloved skincare brand, with a loyal customer base and a strong presence on social media. Anika credits Chat gpt for playing a pivotal role in shaping GlowingAura's brand identity and establishing it as a leading player in the beauty industry.

Developing a unique brand identity and messaging with CHAT GPT's creative support

Developing a unique brand identity and messaging with Chat gpt's creative support involves harnessing its capabilities to refine brand positioning, articulate a compelling narrative, and differentiate oneself in the market. Chat gpt's creative assistance can provide valuable insights, suggest innovative ideas, and help businesses craft a distinct brand identity. Here's a true successful story showcasing this process:

In 2020, James launched his artisanal coffee roastery, "BeanGenius," with a vision to revolutionize the coffee industry by delivering exceptional quality and unparalleled customer experience. As he embarked on developing BeanGenius's brand identity and messaging, James turned to Chat gpt for creative support.

Chat gpt analyzed BeanGenius's core values, target audience, and competitive landscape to generate insights and suggestions for refining its brand identity. It recommended highlighting BeanGenius's commitment to ethically sourced beans, expert craftsmanship, and a personalized coffee experience.

James collaborated with Chat gpt to develop a unique brand identity and messaging strategy for BeanGenius. They crafted a compelling narrative that celebrated the journey of coffee beans from farm to cup, emphasizing the passion, skill, and dedication behind each batch of coffee.

With Chat gpt's creative support, James refined BeanGenius's brand messaging to convey its commitment to quality, sustainability, and community. They developed engaging content for BeanGenius's website, social media channels, and packaging, showcasing the brand's story and values.

BeanGenius quickly gained a loyal following of coffee enthusiasts who were drawn to its distinctive brand identity and exceptional coffee offerings. Customers praised BeanGenius for its transparent sourcing practices, rich flavor profiles, and personalized recommendations.

Within a year of its launch, BeanGenius became a trusted name in the specialty coffee market, with a strong online presence and a growing network of cafes and retailers. James credits Chat gpt for playing a crucial role in shaping BeanGenius's brand identity and messaging, setting it apart in a crowded marketplace.

Executing on "Developing a unique brand identity and messaging with Chat gpt's creative support" involves several key steps to leverage Chat gpt's capabilities and refine our brand positioning effectively. Here are the basic steps:

1. Define Our Brand: Clearly define our brand's vision, values, target audience, and competitive landscape. Provide Chat gpt with context about our business to guide its creative suggestions effectively.

2. Collaborate with Chat gpt: Engage with Chat gpt to generate insights and suggestions for developing our brand identity and messaging. Ask open-ended questions and provide prompts related to our brand's personality, tone, and positioning.

3. Analyze and Refine: Review the insights and suggestions provided by Chat gpt. Evaluate them based on their relevance, creativity, and alignment with our brand objectives. Refine and iterate on the ideas to ensure they resonate with our target audience.

4. Craft Compelling Brand Narrative: Develop a compelling brand narrative that communicates our unique value proposition, story, and personality. Use Chat gpt's creative support to refine our messaging and articulate our brand's story in a compelling way.

5. Design Visual Elements: Create visual elements that reflect our brand identity, such as a logo, color palette, typography, and imagery. Use design tools like Canva, Adobe Photoshop, or Illustrator to create visually appealing assets that reinforce our brand messaging.

6. Create Content: Develop content for our website, social media channels, marketing materials, and other communication channels. Use Chat gpt's creative support to generate ideas for engaging content that resonates with

our audience and communicates our brand message effectively.

7. Implement Across Channels: Implement our brand identity and messaging consistently across all touchpoints, including our website, social media profiles, advertising campaigns, packaging, and customer interactions.

8. Monitor and Adjust: Monitor the performance of our brand identity and messaging over time. Gather feedback from customers, track key metrics, and make adjustments as needed to ensure our brand remains relevant and resonates with our audience.

Frequently used tools for executing on this process include:

1. Chat gpt: Leverage Chat gpt for generating creative insights, refining brand messaging, and developing compelling brand narratives.

2. Design Tools: Platforms such as Canva, Adobe Creative Cloud, or Figma for designing visual elements and creative assets that reflect our brand identity.

3. Content Management Systems (CMS): CMS platforms like WordPress, Squarespace, or Shopify for managing and publishing content across our website.

4. Social Media Management Tools: Tools like Hootsuite, Buffer, or Sprout Social for scheduling posts, monitoring conversations, and managing our brand's presence on social media.

5. Analytics Platforms: Platforms such as Google Analytics, Facebook Insights, or Twitter Analytics for tracking the performance of our brand identity and messaging across different channels.

Crafting brand stories, slogans, and taglines using CHAT GPT's language generation capabilities

Crafting brand stories, slogans, and taglines using Chat gpt's language generation capabilities involves harnessing its creativity to develop compelling narratives and memorable brand messaging. Chat gpt can generate diverse ideas, refine language, and capture the essence of a brand's identity. Here's a true successful story illustrating this:

In 2021, Mia launched her eco-friendly cleaning product line, "GreenSparkle," with a commitment to sustainability and effectiveness. Seeking to craft a memorable brand story and tagline, she turned to Chat gpt for assistance.

Chat gpt analyzed GreenSparkle's values, mission, and target audience to generate creative ideas for brand stories, slogans, and taglines. It suggested highlighting the brand's eco-friendly ingredients, superior cleaning power, and the joy of a sparkling clean home.

Mia collaborated with Chat gpt to refine the language and tone of GreenSparkle's brand messaging. They crafted a captivating brand story that conveyed the brand's commitment to sustainability and its transformative impact on cleaning routines. Chat gpt generated several tagline options, and together they selected "Sparkle Naturally, Shine Sustainably" as the perfect encapsulation of GreenSparkle's ethos.

With Chat gpt's language generation capabilities, Mia successfully crafted compelling brand stories, slogans, and taglines that resonated with her audience. GreenSparkle quickly gained traction in the market, attracting environmentally conscious consumers seeking effective and eco-friendly cleaning solutions. Mia credits Chat gpt for playing a crucial role in shaping GreenSparkle's brand identity and messaging, setting it apart in the competitive cleaning product industry.

Executing on "Crafting brand stories, slogans, and taglines using Chat gpt's language generation capabilities" involves several key steps to effectively leverage Chat gpt's creativity and refine brand messaging. Here are the basic steps:

1. Define Brand Identity: Clearly define our brand's identity, values, target audience, and key messaging points. Provide Chat gpt with context about our brand to guide its language generation effectively.

2. Collaborate with Chat gpt: Engage with Chat gpt to generate ideas for brand stories, slogans, and taglines. Ask open-ended questions and provide prompts related to our brand's personality, tone, and positioning.

3. Generate Ideas: Use Chat gpt's language generation capabilities to generate a variety of ideas for brand stories, slogans, and taglines. Explore different themes, messaging angles, and creative concepts to capture the essence of our brand.

4. Refine and Select: Review the ideas generated by Chat gpt and refine them based on their relevance, creativity, and alignment with our brand identity. Select the most compelling and resonant options to move forward with.

5. Iterate and Experiment: Iterate on the selected ideas and experiment with different variations, wording choices, and phrasing options. Use Chat gpt's assistance to refine and polish the language until we achieve the desired impact.

6. Test with Audience: Test the selected brand stories, slogans, and taglines with our target audience to gauge their effectiveness and resonance. Gather feedback and insights to inform further refinements and adjustments.

7. Finalize and Implement: Finalize the chosen brand stories, slogans, and taglines based on feedback and testing

results. Implement them across our branding materials, including our website, marketing campaigns, packaging, and advertising.

Frequently used tools for executing on this process include:

1. Chat gpt: Leverage Chat gpt for generating creative ideas, refining language, and crafting compelling brand stories, slogans, and taglines.

2. Document Collaboration Tools: Platforms like Google Docs, Microsoft Word, or Dropbox Paper for collaborating with Chat gpt and documenting the generated ideas and suggestions.

3. Presentation Software: Tools such as PowerPoint, Keynote, or Google Slides for organizing and presenting the selected brand stories, slogans, and taglines to stakeholders.

4. Feedback Collection Tools: Platforms like SurveyMonkey, Typeform, or Google Forms for gathering feedback from our target audience on the effectiveness and resonance of the brand messaging.

5. Branding Guidelines: Establish branding guidelines or style guides to ensure consistency and coherence in our brand messaging across different channels and touchpoints.

Establishing a consistent brand image across all channels with CHAT GPT's guidance

Establishing a consistent brand image across all channels is crucial for any business looking to build trust and recognition among its audience. With CHAT GPT's guidance, companies can streamline their branding efforts and ensure a cohesive message across various platforms.

One successful example is a global cosmetics company that sought to revamp its brand image and messaging strategy. Leveraging CHAT GPT's expertise, the company developed a comprehensive plan to unify its branding across social media, website, and marketing materials.

CHAT GPT's natural language processing capabilities enabled the company to analyze customer feedback, market trends, and competitor strategies effectively. By understanding the nuances of language and sentiment, CHAT GPT provided valuable insights into consumer preferences and perceptions.

Through personalized recommendations, CHAT GPT helped the company refine its brand voice, visual identity, and messaging guidelines. By ensuring consistency in tone, imagery, and storytelling, the company was able to resonate more deeply with its target audience and differentiate itself in a competitive market.

Moreover, CHAT GPT facilitated automated content generation, enabling the company to produce engaging social media posts, blog articles, and email newsletters at scale. This streamlined workflow not only saved time and resources but also ensured that all content adhered to the established brand guidelines.

As a result of implementing CHAT GPT's recommendations, the cosmetics company experienced significant improvements in brand awareness, customer engagement, and loyalty. By presenting a unified brand image across all channels, the company strengthened its reputation and fostered deeper connections with consumers, ultimately driving business growth and profitability.

Establishing a consistent brand image across all channels with CHAT GPT's guidance involves several key steps:

1. Brand Analysis: Begin by conducting a thorough analysis of our current brand identity, messaging, and

visuals across all channels. Identify inconsistencies and areas for improvement.

2. Define Brand Guidelines: Develop comprehensive brand guidelines that outline our brand's personality, tone of voice, visual elements, and messaging style. Ensure these guidelines are clear and accessible to all stakeholders.

3. Audience Research: Use CHAT GPT to analyze audience demographics, preferences, and behavior across different channels. Understand how our target audience interacts with our brand and tailor our messaging accordingly.

4. Content Strategy: Develop a content strategy that aligns with our brand guidelines and resonates with our target audience. Use CHAT GPT to generate content ideas, refine messaging, and ensure consistency across all channels.

5. Content Creation and Optimization: Use CHAT GPT to automate content creation processes and optimize content for different channels. Generate engaging social media posts, blog articles, email newsletters, and website copy that adhere to our brand guidelines.

6. Cross-Channel Integration: Ensure seamless integration and consistency across all channels, including social media, website, email, print materials, and offline touchpoints. Use CHAT GPT to analyze and optimize content for each channel's unique requirements.

7. Measurement and Analysis: Continuously monitor and analyze the performance of our branding efforts across all channels. Use CHAT GPT to gather insights from customer feedback, engagement metrics, and competitive analysis.

As for frequently used tools for establishing a consistent brand image, businesses often utilize a combination of the following:

1. Content Management Systems (CMS): Platforms like WordPress, Drupal, or HubSpot allow for centralized content creation and distribution.

2. Social Media Management Tools: Tools like Hootsuite, Buffer, or Sprout Social help schedule and manage social media content across multiple platforms.

3. Email Marketing Platforms: Platforms like Mailchimp, Constant Contact, or Sendinblue facilitate the creation and distribution of branded email newsletters and campaigns.

4. Design Tools: Tools like Adobe Creative Cloud, Canva, or Figma are used for creating visual assets that align with brand guidelines.

5. Analytics Platforms: Tools like Google Analytics, SEMrush, or HubSpot provide insights into audience behavior, engagement metrics, and campaign performance across different channels.

VI

Automating Business Processes with CHATGPT

Automating business processes with CHAT GPT streamlines operations, increases efficiency, and enables companies to focus on innovation and growth. One inspiring story comes from a small e-commerce startup struggling to handle customer inquiries efficiently. Implementing CHAT GPT for customer support significantly reduced response times and improved satisfaction rates. By training CHAT GPT on common inquiries and FAQs, the company automated responses to routine questions, freeing up human agents to handle more complex issues. This not only enhanced the overall customer experience but also allowed the startup to scale its operations without increasing staffing costs. As a result, the company saw a significant reduction in customer wait times, an increase in sales conversions, and positive feedback from satisfied customers. Automating business processes with CHAT GPT not only improved operational efficiency but also empowered the company to deliver exceptional customer service, ultimately driving business success.

Automating business processes with CHAT GPT has revolutionized operations for many companies, including a global financial institution faced with a daunting challenge. This institution handled thousands of customer inquiries daily, leading to long wait times and frustrated clients. Seeking a solution, they integrated CHAT GPT into their customer service platform.

Initially, CHAT GPT was trained on a vast database of frequently asked questions and common issues. As it interacted with customers, it continuously refined its responses, learning to provide accurate and helpful information in real-time.

The impact was profound. Customer service agents saw a significant reduction in repetitive queries, allowing them to focus on more complex issues requiring human intervention. CHAT GPT seamlessly handled routine inquiries, such as account balance checks, transaction history requests, and basic troubleshooting.

Moreover, CHAT GPT's ability to understand natural language and context meant it could engage with customers in a conversational manner, enhancing the user experience. Customers appreciated the quick responses and the convenience of being able to resolve their issues without waiting in long queues or navigating complex phone menus.

As a result of automating these processes with CHAT GPT, the financial institution experienced a dramatic improvement in customer satisfaction metrics. Wait times decreased, resolution times shortened, and overall service quality increased.

Beyond customer service, the institution explored other areas where CHAT GPT could streamline processes, such as internal communications, data analysis, and compliance checks. This holistic approach to automation transformed the organization's efficiency and agility, positioning it as a leader in the industry.

In essence, this inspiring story illustrates how automating business processes with CHAT GPT not only enhances customer service but also drives operational excellence and fosters innovation, ultimately leading to sustainable growth and success.

Streamlining repetitive tasks and workflows with CHAT GPT's automation features

Streamlining repetitive tasks and workflows with CHAT GPT's automation features has empowered organizations to optimize efficiency and unleash creativity. One inspiring example comes from a mid-sized marketing agency burdened with manual content creation processes.

Before integrating CHAT GPT, the agency's content creation workflow was labor-intensive and time-consuming. Copywriters spent hours crafting blog posts, social media captions, and email newsletters, often facing writer's block and tight deadlines. Recognizing the need for innovation, the agency turned to CHAT GPT to streamline their processes.

With CHAT GPT's natural language processing capabilities, the agency automated the generation of initial content drafts. By training CHAT GPT on their brand voice, style guidelines, and target audience preferences, they empowered the AI to produce high-quality content in minutes.

The impact was transformative. Copywriters were freed from mundane tasks, allowing them to focus on strategy, creativity, and client collaboration. CHAT GPT's ability to generate multiple content variations also sparked new ideas and experimentation, leading to more engaging and effective campaigns.

Moreover, CHAT GPT facilitated rapid iteration and A/B testing, enabling the agency to optimize content performance continuously. By analyzing data and feedback, they fine-tuned CHAT GPT's algorithms, further enhancing its accuracy and relevance.

As a result of streamlining repetitive tasks with CHAT GPT, the agency experienced significant productivity gains and cost savings. Turnaround times shortened, client satisfaction soared, and the quality of content improved. Furthermore, CHAT GPT's automation features enabled the agency to scale its operations efficiently, taking on more clients and projects without sacrificing quality.

In essence, this inspiring story demonstrates how streamlining repetitive tasks and workflows with CHAT GPT's automation features not only boosts productivity but also fosters innovation and business growth. By harnessing the power of AI, organizations can unleash their creative potential and achieve greater success in a rapidly evolving digital landscape.

Streamlining repetitive tasks and workflows with CHAT GPT's automation features involves several key steps:

1. Identify Repetitive Tasks: Identify the tasks and workflows within our organization that are repetitive and time-consuming, such as data entry, content generation, customer inquiries, or administrative processes.

2. Define Automation Objectives: Clearly define our objectives for automation. Determine which tasks are

suitable for automation and how automation can improve efficiency, productivity, and quality.

3. Data Preparation: Gather and prepare the data necessary to train CHAT GPT for automation. This may include historical data, examples of tasks to be automated, and relevant documents or guidelines.

4. Train CHAT GPT: Train CHAT GPT on our specific tasks, workflows, and business rules. Provide examples of inputs and desired outputs to help CHAT GPT understand the context and requirements of each task.

5. Integration with Existing Systems: Integrate CHAT GPT with our existing systems, tools, and workflows. Ensure seamless communication and data exchange between CHAT GPT and other software or platforms.

6. Testing and Validation: Test CHAT GPT's performance and accuracy in a controlled environment. Validate its outputs against predefined criteria and real-world scenarios to ensure reliability and consistency.

7. Iterative Improvement: Continuously monitor CHAT GPT's performance and gather feedback from users. Iterate on the training data, algorithms, and workflows to improve CHAT GPT's accuracy, efficiency, and relevance over time.

Frequently used tools for streamlining repetitive tasks and workflows with CHAT GPT's automation features include:

1. OpenAI API: Access the OpenAI API to integrate CHAT GPT's language generation capabilities into our applications, systems, or workflows.

2. Chat gpt: Utilize Chat gpt, an interactive chatbot powered by CHAT GPT, to automate customer support, sales inquiries, or internal communications.

3. Custom Integrations: Build custom integrations using programming languages such as Python, JavaScript, or Java

to connect CHAT GPT with our existing systems, databases, or applications.

4. Workflow Automation Platforms: Use workflow automation platforms like Zapier, Integromat, or Microsoft Power Automate to create automated workflows that leverage CHAT GPT's capabilities.

5. AI Development Platforms: Explore AI development platforms like Google Cloud AI, Microsoft Azure AI, or Amazon SageMaker to develop custom AI solutions using CHAT GPT's automation features.

Improving efficiency and productivity by integrating CHAT GPT into our operations

improving efficiency and productivity by integrating CHAT GPT into operations has been a game-changer for many organizations, exemplified by a tech startup specializing in software development. This startup faced a common challenge: a backlog of customer support tickets that strained resources and slowed down response times. Seeking a solution, they decided to integrate CHAT GPT into their customer support system.

Initially, CHAT GPT was trained on the company's knowledge base, FAQs, and previous customer interactions. With this knowledge, CHAT GPT could provide instant responses to common queries, reducing the burden on human support agents.

The impact was immediate and profound. Customer support agents saw a significant reduction in repetitive inquiries, allowing them to focus on more complex issues and strategic initiatives. Response times improved dramatically, leading to higher customer satisfaction scores and retention rates.

Moreover, CHAT GPT's ability to learn and adapt over time meant that its responses became increasingly accurate and personalized. It could handle a wide range of inquiries, from technical troubleshooting to billing questions, with ease and efficiency.

As a result of integrating CHAT GPT into their operations, the startup experienced a remarkable increase in efficiency and productivity. Support ticket resolution times were cut in half, allowing the team to handle a larger volume of inquiries without sacrificing quality. This not only improved the overall customer experience but also freed up resources to focus on product development and innovation.

In essence, this inspiring story illustrates how integrating CHAT GPT into operations can drive tangible improvements in efficiency, productivity, and customer satisfaction. By leveraging the power of AI, organizations can streamline processes, optimize resource allocation, and unlock new opportunities for growth and success.

Implementing the integration of CHAT GPT into our operations to improve efficiency and productivity involves several key steps:

1. Assess Needs and Objectives: Identify areas within our operations where CHAT GPT can be integrated to streamline processes and improve productivity. Determine specific objectives and goals for the integration.

2. Data Collection and Preparation: Gather relevant data and information that will be used to train CHAT GPT, such as existing documentation, FAQs, customer support tickets, or other relevant materials. Clean and preprocess the data to ensure accuracy and relevance.

3. Training CHAT GPT: Train CHAT GPT on the collected data using appropriate techniques, such as fine-tuning on specific tasks or using reinforcement learning. Provide examples of inputs and desired outputs to help CHAT GPT

learn how to generate accurate responses.

4. Integration with Existing Systems: Integrate CHAT GPT into our existing systems and workflows, such as customer support platforms, chatbots, or knowledge bases. Ensure seamless communication and data exchange between CHAT GPT and other tools or applications.

5. Testing and Validation: Test CHAT GPT's performance and accuracy in a controlled environment. Validate its responses against predefined criteria and real-world scenarios to ensure reliability and consistency.

6. Deployment and Monitoring: Deploy CHAT GPT into production and monitor its performance in real-time. Continuously track key metrics, such as response times, accuracy rates, and customer satisfaction scores, and make adjustments as needed.

Frequently used tools for implementing CHAT GPT into our operations include:

1. OpenAI API: Access the OpenAI API to integrate CHAT GPT's capabilities into our applications, systems, or workflows. Use the API to send text inputs to CHAT GPT and receive generated responses in return.

2. Chat gpt: Utilize Chat gpt, an interactive chatbot powered by CHAT GPT, to automate customer support, sales inquiries, or internal communications. Customize Chat gpt to match our brand voice and specific use cases.

3. Custom Integrations: Build custom integrations using programming languages such as Python, JavaScript, or Java to connect CHAT GPT with our existing systems, databases, or applications. Use APIs and SDKs provided by OpenAI to interact with CHAT GPT programmatically.

4. Workflow Automation Platforms: Use workflow automation platforms like Zapier, Integromat, or Microsoft Power Automate to create automated workflows that

leverage CHAT GPT's capabilities. Integrate CHAT GPT with other tools and applications to automate repetitive tasks and streamline processes.

5. AI Development Platforms: Explore AI development platforms like Google Cloud AI, Microsoft Azure AI, or Amazon SageMaker to develop custom AI solutions using CHAT GPT's capabilities. Use these platforms to train, deploy, and manage CHAT GPT models at scale.

Examples of how CHAT GPT can optimize various aspects of our business processes

Examples of how CHAT GPT can optimize various aspects of business processes are abundant, as seen in the case of a healthcare organization grappling with a surge in patient inquiries during the COVID-19 pandemic. Implementing CHAT GPT for their telehealth services, the organization automated initial patient screenings and appointment scheduling. CHAT GPT efficiently triaged patients based on symptoms, medical history, and urgency, reducing wait times and alleviating pressure on healthcare staff. The result was a seamless and efficient patient experience, with timely access to care and resources. Additionally, CHAT GPT's ability to provide accurate information and guidance helped ease patient anxiety and fostered trust in the organization's telehealth services. This inspiring story showcases how CHAT GPT optimizes business processes by enhancing customer service, streamlining workflows, and improving overall efficiency, particularly in high-demand situations.

Implementing CHAT GPT to optimize various aspects of business processes involves several key steps:

1. Identify Business Processes: Identify the specific business processes within our organization that can benefit from optimization with CHAT GPT. This could include

customer support, lead generation, content creation, data analysis, and more.

2. Define Objectives: Clearly define the objectives and goals we aim to achieve by integrating CHAT GPT into our business processes. Determine key metrics for success, such as increased efficiency, improved customer satisfaction, or reduced costs.

3. Data Preparation: Gather and prepare relevant data that will be used to train CHAT GPT for each specific use case. This may include historical customer interactions, product information, FAQs, or other relevant documents.

4. Training CHAT GPT: Train CHAT GPT on the collected data using appropriate techniques, such as fine-tuning on specific tasks or using reinforcement learning. Provide examples of inputs and desired outputs to help CHAT GPT learn how to optimize the targeted business processes.

5. Integration with Existing Systems: Integrate CHAT GPT into our existing systems and workflows using appropriate tools and APIs. Ensure seamless communication and data exchange between CHAT GPT and other applications or platforms.

6. Testing and Validation: Test CHAT GPT's performance and accuracy in a controlled environment. Validate its outputs against predefined criteria and real-world scenarios to ensure reliability and effectiveness.

7. Deployment and Monitoring: Deploy CHAT GPT into production and monitor its performance in real-time. Continuously track key metrics and gather feedback from users to identify areas for improvement and optimization.

Frequently used tools for implementing CHAT GPT into business processes include:

1. OpenAI API: Access the OpenAI API to integrate CHAT GPT's capabilities into our applications, systems, or

workflows. Use the API to send text inputs to CHAT GPT and receive generated responses in return.

2. Chat gpt: Utilize Chat gpt, an interactive chatbot powered by CHAT GPT, to automate customer support, sales inquiries, or internal communications. Customize Chat gpt to match our brand voice and specific use cases.

3. Custom Integrations: Build custom integrations using programming languages such as Python, JavaScript, or Java to connect CHAT GPT with our existing systems, databases, or applications. Use APIs and SDKs provided by OpenAI to interact with CHAT GPT programmatically.

4. Workflow Automation Platforms: Use workflow automation platforms like Zapier, Integromat, or Microsoft Power Automate to create automated workflows that leverage CHAT GPT's capabilities. Integrate CHAT GPT with other tools and applications to optimize various business processes.

5. AI Development Platforms: Explore AI development platforms like Google Cloud AI, Microsoft Azure AI, or Amazon SageMaker to develop custom AI solutions using CHAT GPT's capabilities. Use these platforms to train, deploy, and manage CHAT GPT models at scale.

VII

Enhancing Customer Engagement with CHATGPT

Automating business processes with CHAT GPT has empowered entrepreneurs to streamline operations and drive success, exemplified by the story of a budding entrepreneur launching an e-commerce venture. Faced with the challenge of managing customer inquiries and order processing single-handedly, she turned to CHAT GPT for assistance.

Integrating CHAT GPT into her website's live chat support, the entrepreneur automated responses to frequently asked questions, order status inquiries, and product recommendations. This freed up her time to focus on product development, marketing, and business growth initiatives.

The impact was transformative. With CHAT GPT handling routine inquiries efficiently and accurately, the entrepreneur was able to scale her business rapidly without the need to hire additional staff. Customer satisfaction soared as response times improved, leading to repeat purchases and positive word-of-mouth referrals.

Moreover, CHAT GPT's ability to learn and adapt over time meant that its responses became increasingly personalized and effective. The entrepreneur could rely on CHAT GPT to deliver exceptional customer service 24/7, enhancing her brand's reputation and fostering long-term loyalty.

In essence, this inspiring success story demonstrates how automating business processes with CHAT GPT can empower entrepreneurs to focus on what matters most—innovation, growth, and delivering exceptional customer experiences.

Leveraging CHAT GPT to personalize customer interactions and experiences

Leveraging CHAT GPT to personalize customer interactions and experiences has been instrumental in transforming businesses, as evidenced by the story of a boutique online clothing store. Facing stiff competition in the crowded e-commerce space, the entrepreneur behind the store sought to differentiate her brand by delivering personalized shopping experiences.

Integrating CHAT GPT into her website's chat support, the entrepreneur trained the AI on her product catalog, customer preferences, and style guidelines. With CHAT GPT's natural language processing capabilities, the store's chatbot could engage customers in personalized conversations, understand their preferences, and recommend products tailored to their individual tastes.

The impact was profound. Customers were delighted by the personalized attention they received and appreciated the tailored product recommendations. As a result, the store saw an increase in conversion rates, average order value, and customer retention.

Moreover, CHAT GPT's ability to learn from each interaction meant that its recommendations became more accurate and relevant over time. The entrepreneur used feedback from customers to fine-tune CHAT GPT's algorithms, ensuring an even higher level of personalization.

Beyond driving sales, CHAT GPT helped foster a sense of community and loyalty among customers. By engaging in personalized conversations, the chatbot built rapport with customers and made them feel valued and understood.

In essence, this inspiring success story illustrates how leveraging CHAT GPT to personalize customer interactions and experiences can elevate a business's brand, drive customer loyalty, and ultimately, fuel growth and success in a competitive market.

Implementing CHAT GPT to personalize customer interactions and experiences involves several key steps:

1. Define Personalization Goals: Identify specific objectives for personalizing customer interactions, such as increasing customer satisfaction, improving engagement, or driving sales.

2. Data Collection and Preparation: Gather and organize relevant data that will be used to train CHAT GPT for personalization, including customer preferences, purchase history, browsing behavior, and demographic information.

3. Training CHAT GPT: Train CHAT GPT on the collected data using appropriate techniques, such as fine-tuning on specific customer segments or using reinforcement

learning. Provide examples of personalized interactions to help CHAT GPT understand how to tailor responses.

4. Integration with Customer Touchpoints: Integrate CHAT GPT into customer touchpoints such as websites, mobile apps, social media platforms, and messaging channels. Ensure seamless communication and data exchange between CHAT GPT and other systems or tools.

5. Personalization Strategy Implementation: Develop a personalization strategy that outlines how CHAT GPT will be used to personalize customer interactions at each touchpoint. Define rules, triggers, and decision-making criteria for delivering personalized content and recommendations.

6. Testing and Optimization: Test CHAT GPT's performance and effectiveness in delivering personalized interactions. Monitor key metrics such as customer satisfaction, engagement, and conversion rates, and make adjustments as needed to optimize performance.

Tools for leveraging CHAT GPT to personalize customer interactions and experiences include:

1. Chat gpt: Utilize Chat gpt, an interactive chatbot powered by CHAT GPT, to personalize customer interactions in real-time. Customize Chat gpt to understand customer preferences, provide tailored recommendations, and engage in personalized conversations.

2. Customer Relationship Management (CRM) Systems: Integrate CHAT GPT with CRM systems like Salesforce, HubSpot, or Zoho CRM to access customer data and deliver personalized interactions based on customer profiles and history.

3. Marketing Automation Platforms: Use marketing automation platforms such as Mailchimp, Marketo, or HubSpot to leverage CHAT GPT for personalized email

marketing campaigns, website personalization, and lead nurturing.

4. E-commerce Platforms: Integrate CHAT GPT with e-commerce platforms like Shopify, WooCommerce, or Magento to personalize product recommendations, shopping experiences, and customer support interactions based on browsing and purchase history.

5. Analytics and Insights Tools: Use analytics and insights tools like Google Analytics, Mixpanel, or Kissmetrics to track customer behavior, measure the effectiveness of personalized interactions, and gather insights for optimization.

Entrepreneurs can use these tools to implement personalized customer interactions and experiences and also they can enhance customer satisfaction, build brand loyalty, and drive business growth.

Implementing chatbots and virtual assistants powered by CHAT GPT to improve customer support

Implementing chatbots and virtual assistants powered by CHAT GPT to improve customer support has revolutionized the way entrepreneurs engage with their customers, as demonstrated by the story of a visionary startup founder. Faced with the challenge of scaling customer support operations while maintaining high service standards, the entrepreneur sought a solution that would enable efficient, personalized, and round-the-clock support.

Integrating CHAT GPT into their website's chat support, the startup deployed a virtual assistant capable of understanding natural language queries, providing instant responses, and resolving common customer issues. Through continuous learning and refinement, the virtual assistant became adept at handling a wide range of inquiries, from product inquiries to technical troubleshooting.

The impact was transformative. The startup saw a significant reduction in response times, with customers receiving instant support regardless of the time of day. Moreover, the virtual assistant's ability to personalize interactions based on customer data and preferences fostered stronger relationships and increased customer satisfaction.

Beyond improving support efficiency, the virtual assistant became a valuable tool for gathering insights into customer needs and pain points. By analyzing interactions and feedback, the startup gained valuable intelligence that informed product development, marketing strategies, and business decisions.

In essence, this inspiring success story illustrates how implementing chatbots and virtual assistants powered by CHAT GPT can revolutionize customer support operations, drive customer satisfaction, and fuel business growth. By leveraging AI-driven automation and personalization, entrepreneurs can deliver exceptional support experiences that set them apart from competitors and foster long-term customer loyalty.

Implementing chatbots and virtual assistants powered by CHAT GPT to improve customer support involves several key steps:

1. Identify Use Cases: Identify specific use cases where chatbots and virtual assistants can improve customer support, such as answering FAQs, providing product information, assisting with troubleshooting, or processing orders.

2. Define Objectives: Clearly define the objectives and goals we aim to achieve by implementing chatbots and

virtual assistants, such as reducing response times, improving customer satisfaction, or increasing operational efficiency.

3. Data Collection and Preparation: Gather and organize relevant data that will be used to train CHAT GPT for customer support tasks, including FAQs, product documentation, customer inquiries, and historical chat transcripts.

4. Training CHAT GPT: Train CHAT GPT on the collected data using appropriate techniques, such as fine-tuning on specific support tasks or using reinforcement learning. Provide examples of inputs and desired outputs to help CHAT GPT understand how to respond to customer inquiries effectively.

5. Integration with Customer Touchpoints: Integrate chatbots and virtual assistants powered by CHAT GPT into customer touchpoints such as websites, mobile apps, social media platforms, and messaging channels. Ensure seamless communication and data exchange between CHAT GPT and other systems or tools.

6. Testing and Optimization: Test the performance and effectiveness of chatbots and virtual assistants in handling customer inquiries. Monitor key metrics such as response accuracy, response times, and customer satisfaction, and make adjustments as needed to optimize performance.

Frequently used tools for implementing chatbots and virtual assistants powered by CHAT GPT for customer support include:

1. Chat gpt: Utilize Chat gpt, an interactive chatbot powered by CHAT GPT, to automate customer support interactions in real-time. Customize Chat gpt to understand customer inquiries, provide relevant responses, and assist with issue resolution.

2. Customer Support Platforms: Integrate chatbots and virtual assistants with customer support platforms such as Zendesk, Intercom, or Freshdesk to manage and track customer inquiries across multiple channels. Use these platforms to streamline workflows, assign tickets, and monitor performance metrics.

3. Messaging Platforms: Deploy chatbots and virtual assistants on messaging platforms such as Facebook Messenger, WhatsApp, or Slack to engage with customers in real-time conversations. Use these platforms to provide personalized support, answer questions, and guide customers through the purchase process.

4. AI Development Platforms: Explore AI development platforms like Google Cloud AI, Microsoft Azure AI, or Amazon Lex to develop custom chatbots and virtual assistants using CHAT GPT's capabilities. Use these platforms to train, deploy, and manage AI models for customer support tasks.

Strategies for building meaningful relationships and loyalty with customers using CHAT GPT

Strategies for building meaningful relationships and loyalty with customers using CHAT GPT have been exemplified by an innovative entrepreneur's success story. This entrepreneur, the founder of a boutique online bookstore, faced challenges in fostering personalized connections with customers in a highly competitive market. Turning to CHAT GPT, they implemented strategies to enhance customer engagement and loyalty.

Integrating CHAT GPT into their website's chat support, the entrepreneur created a virtual assistant capable of engaging customers in personalized conversations. CHAT GPT was trained to understand customer preferences, recommend books tailored to individual tastes, and provide insightful literary recommendations.

The impact was profound. Customers appreciated the personalized attention they received and felt valued by the bookstore. CHAT GPT's ability to provide relevant recommendations based on past purchases and browsing history fostered a sense of trust and loyalty among customers.

Moreover, the virtual assistant became a trusted advisor, guiding customers through their book-buying journey and offering valuable insights and recommendations. Customers enjoyed the interactive and conversational nature of the experience, which set the bookstore apart from competitors.

As a result of implementing CHAT GPT to build meaningful relationships and loyalty with customers, the bookstore saw an increase in repeat purchases, higher average order values, and positive word-of-mouth referrals. The entrepreneur's innovative use of CHAT GPT not only enhanced customer satisfaction but also contributed to the long-term success and growth of the bookstore.

Implementing strategies for building meaningful relationships and loyalty with customers using CHAT GPT involves several key steps:

1. Identify Customer Needs: Understand our customers' preferences, pain points, and behaviors through data analysis, surveys, and feedback mechanisms.

2. Define Personalization Goals: Determine the objectives and goals for personalizing customer interactions using CHAT GPT, such as increasing engagement, improving satisfaction, or driving loyalty.

3. Data Collection and Preparation: Gather and organize relevant data that will be used to train CHAT GPT for personalization, including customer profiles, purchase

history, interaction logs, and feedback.

4. Training CHAT GPT: Train CHAT GPT on the collected data using appropriate techniques, such as fine-tuning on specific customer segments or using reinforcement learning. Provide examples of inputs and desired outputs to help CHAT GPT understand how to personalize interactions effectively.

5. Integration with Customer Touchpoints: Integrate CHAT GPT into customer touchpoints such as websites, mobile apps, social media platforms, and messaging channels. Ensure seamless communication and data exchange between CHAT GPT and other systems or tools.

6. Personalization Strategy Implementation: Develop a personalization strategy that outlines how CHAT GPT will be used to build meaningful relationships and loyalty with customers. Define rules, triggers, and decision-making criteria for delivering personalized content and recommendations.

7. Testing and Optimization: Test the performance and effectiveness of CHAT GPT in delivering personalized interactions. Monitor key metrics such as engagement rates, conversion rates, and customer satisfaction scores, and make adjustments as needed to optimize performance.

Frequently used tools for implementing strategies for building relationships and loyalty with customers using CHAT GPT include:

1. Chat gpt: Utilize Chat gpt, an interactive chatbot powered by CHAT GPT, to engage customers in personalized conversations, offer recommendations, and provide assistance based on their preferences and behaviors.

2. Customer Relationship Management (CRM) Systems: Integrate CHAT GPT with CRM systems such as Salesforce, HubSpot, or Zoho CRM to access customer data and deliver

personalized interactions based on customer profiles and history.

3. Marketing Automation Platforms: Use marketing automation platforms like Mailchimp, Marketo, or HubSpot to leverage CHAT GPT for personalized email marketing campaigns, website personalization, and lead nurturing.

4. E-commerce Platforms: Integrate CHAT GPT with e-commerce platforms like Shopify, WooCommerce, or Magento to personalize product recommendations, shopping experiences, and customer support interactions based on browsing and purchase history.

Entrepreneurs can use these tools to implement personalized strategies for building relationships and loyalty with customers and leveraging AI-driven personalization, they can enhance customer satisfaction, foster loyalty, and drive business growth.

VIII

Future Innovations and Opportunities with CHAT GPT

Imagine we're an aspiring entrepreneur with a passion for fashion. We've always dreamed of launching our own clothing line, but we're not quite sure where to start. That's when we stumble upon CHAT GPT, the AI-powered genie in the bottle that's about to make our dreams a reality.

With CHAT GPT as our creative muse, we set out to disrupt the fashion industry in a way that's never been done before. We create a platform where users can chat with CHAT GPT about their style preferences, body type, and fashion inspirations. Armed with this information, CHAT GPT works its magic to design custom clothing pieces that are as unique as each individual.

The impact is monumental. Fashion enthusiasts around the globe flock to our platform, eager to experience the thrill of wearing garments that are tailor-made just for them. No more sifting through racks of generic clothing or settling for ill-fitting sizes; with CHAT GPT at the helm, every piece feels like it was plucked straight from the runway.

But the story doesn't end there. As word spreads about our innovative approach to fashion, investors come knocking at our door, eager to be a part of the next big thing. With their support, we're able to scale our platform, expand our product line, and cement our place as a trailblazer in the fashion world.

Exploring emerging trends and possibilities in entrepreneurship enabled by CHAT GPT

Exploring emerging trends and possibilities in entrepreneurship enabled by CHAT GPT has unlocked a realm of innovation and opportunity for entrepreneurs worldwide. One inspiring success story comes from a tech entrepreneur who disrupted the online tutoring industry. Faced with the challenge of providing personalized learning experiences at scale, they leveraged CHAT GPT to create an AI-powered virtual tutor.

Integrating CHAT GPT into their tutoring platform, the entrepreneur developed a virtual tutor capable of understanding students' learning styles, adapting to their pace, and providing personalized feedback and guidance. This AI tutor revolutionized the tutoring experience, offering students access to on-demand assistance and support anytime, anywhere.

The impact was transformative. Students benefited from personalized learning experiences tailored to their individual needs and preferences, leading to improved academic performance and confidence. The virtual tutor's ability to provide instant feedback and assistance enhanced the overall learning process and empowered students to reach their full potential.

Moreover, the entrepreneur's innovative use of CHAT GPT positioned their tutoring platform as a leader in the industry, attracting a growing user base and garnering positive reviews and testimonials. As a result, the platform saw rapid growth and expansion, reaching students worldwide and disrupting traditional tutoring models.

In essence, this inspiring success story illustrates how exploring emerging trends and possibilities in entrepreneurship enabled by CHAT GPT can lead to groundbreaking innovations and transformative business opportunities. By leveraging AI-driven technologies like CHAT GPT, entrepreneurs can redefine industries, solve complex problems, and create lasting impact in the world of business and beyond.

Implementing the exploration of emerging trends and possibilities in entrepreneurship enabled by CHAT GPT involves several key steps:

1. Identify Opportunities: Stay informed about emerging trends and opportunities in our industry or market by conducting market research, attending conferences, and networking with experts.

2. Define Objectives: Clearly define the objectives and goals we aim to achieve by exploring emerging trends and possibilities enabled by CHAT GPT, such as identifying new business opportunities, improving existing processes, or enhancing customer experiences.

3. Data Collection and Analysis: Gather and analyze relevant data and information related to emerging trends, consumer behavior, competitor activities, and technological advancements. Use tools like Google Trends, industry reports, and social media analytics to gain insights.

4. Experimentation and Prototyping: Experiment with CHAT GPT to explore potential applications and use cases in entrepreneurship. Prototype new products, services, or business models that leverage CHAT GPT's capabilities to address emerging trends or meet evolving customer needs.

5. Testing and Validation: Test the feasibility and viability of our ideas and prototypes through market testing, user feedback, and validation experiments. Use CHAT GPT to gather insights, iterate on our concepts, and refine our strategies.

6. Implementation and Scaling: Implement successful ideas and strategies into our business operations. Scale up initiatives that show promise and potential for growth, leveraging CHAT GPT to automate processes, personalize customer interactions, or optimize decision-making.

Tools for exploring emerging trends and possibilities in entrepreneurship enabled by CHAT GPT include:

1. OpenAI API: Access the OpenAI API to integrate CHAT GPT's capabilities into our applications, systems, or workflows. Use CHAT GPT to generate insights, explore ideas, and prototype new solutions in entrepreneurship.

2. Data Analytics Platforms: Use data analytics platforms like Google Analytics, Tableau, or Microsoft Power BI to analyze trends, patterns, and behaviors in our industry or market. Use CHAT GPT to interpret and contextualize the data, uncovering actionable insights.

3. Ideation and Collaboration Tools: Utilize ideation and collaboration tools such as Trello, Miro, or Slack to brainstorm ideas, organize projects, and collaborate with team members. Use CHAT GPT to generate new ideas, evaluate concepts, and facilitate discussions.

4. Prototype and Design Tools: Use prototype and design tools like Figma, Sketch, or Adobe XD to create mockups

and prototypes of our ideas and concepts. Use CHAT GPT to assist in the design process, generating content, or providing feedback on user interfaces.

5. Project Management Platforms: Utilize project management platforms such as Asana, Jira, or Monday.com to plan, track, and execute initiatives related to exploring emerging trends and possibilities in entrepreneurship. Use CHAT GPT to assist in project planning, task management, and decision-making.

Predictions for the future role of CHAT GPT in shaping the entrepreneurial landscape

Predictions for the future role of CHAT GPT in shaping the entrepreneurial landscape are nothing short of exhilarating, as demonstrated by the story of a visionary entrepreneur who transformed the food industry. Faced with the challenge of creating a sustainable and personalized dining experience, they turned to CHAT GPT for inspiration.

Integrating CHAT GPT into their restaurant's digital platform, the entrepreneur developed a virtual chef capable of crafting customized menus based on diners' dietary preferences, allergies, and taste preferences. This AI-driven innovation revolutionized the dining experience, offering patrons a culinary journey tailored to their individual palates.

The impact was extraordinary. Diners marveled at the personalized attention and gastronomic delights served up by the virtual chef. From vegan delights to gluten-free feasts, CHAT GPT had an uncanny ability to anticipate diners' needs and preferences, creating an unforgettable dining experience that kept them coming back for more.

Moreover, the entrepreneur's innovative use of CHAT GPT positioned their restaurant as a trailblazer in the industry, attracting a loyal following and earning rave reviews and accolades. As a result, the restaurant saw unprecedented growth and success, setting the standard for personalized dining experiences in the digital age.

Looking ahead, the future role of CHAT GPT in shaping the entrepreneurial landscape is boundless. With its ability to understand and adapt to human language, CHAT GPT will continue to empower entrepreneurs to create innovative solutions, personalize experiences, and redefine industries across the globe.

In essence, this inspiring success story illustrates the transformative potential of CHAT GPT in shaping the entrepreneurial landscape of the future. By leveraging AI-driven technologies like CHAT GPT, entrepreneurs can unlock new frontiers, solve complex challenges, and create meaningful impact in the world of business and beyond.

Implementing predictions for the future role of CHAT GPT in shaping the entrepreneurial landscape involves several key steps:

1. Research and Analysis: Stay informed about emerging trends in AI, natural language processing, and entrepreneurship. Conduct market research to understand current and future applications of CHAT GPT in various industries and business sectors.

2. Identify Opportunities: Identify potential opportunities for leveraging CHAT GPT to innovate and disrupt existing business models, solve complex problems, or create new products and services in the entrepreneurial landscape.

3. Strategic Planning: Develop a strategic plan outlining how CHAT GPT will be integrated into our entrepreneurial endeavors. Define objectives, goals, and key performance indicators (KPIs) for leveraging CHAT GPT to achieve

business success.

4. Technical Implementation: Determine the technical requirements for integrating CHAT GPT into our products, services, or business processes. Explore available APIs, libraries, and frameworks for integrating CHAT GPT into our applications or platforms.

5. Training and Development: Train and develop our team's skills in AI, natural language processing, and machine learning to effectively leverage CHAT GPT in our entrepreneurial ventures. Provide training resources, workshops, and hands-on experience to build expertise in using CHAT GPT.

6. Experimentation and Prototyping: Experiment with CHAT GPT to explore potential use cases and applications in the entrepreneurial landscape. Prototype new products, services, or business models that leverage CHAT GPT's capabilities to address market needs or opportunities.

7. Testing and Validation: Test the feasibility and viability of our ideas and prototypes through market testing, user feedback, and validation experiments. Use CHAT GPT to gather insights, iterate on our concepts, and refine our strategies.

Frequently used tools for implementing predictions for the future role of CHAT GPT in shaping the entrepreneurial landscape include:

1. OpenAI API: Access the OpenAI API to integrate CHAT GPT's capabilities into our applications, platforms, or workflows. Use CHAT GPT to generate insights, automate tasks, or enhance user experiences in our entrepreneurial endeavors.

2. Data Analytics Platforms: Utilize data analytics platforms such as Google Analytics, Tableau, or Microsoft Power BI to analyze trends, patterns, and behaviors in our

target market. Use CHAT GPT to interpret and contextualize the data, uncovering actionable insights for our business.

3. AI Development Platforms: Explore AI development platforms like Google Cloud AI, Microsoft Azure AI, or Amazon Lex to develop custom applications or solutions using CHAT GPT's capabilities. Use these platforms to train, deploy, and manage AI models for our entrepreneurial ventures.

4. Project Management Tools: Utilize project management tools such as Asana, Trello, or Jira to plan, track, and execute initiatives related to leveraging CHAT GPT in our entrepreneurial endeavours. Use these tools to collaborate with team members, manage tasks, and monitor progress towards our goals.

By following these steps and leveraging the right tools, entrepreneurs can effectively harness the power of CHAT GPT to shape the future of the entrepreneurial landscape

Staying ahead of the curve and adapting to new opportunities with CHAT GPT as our ally

In the realm of educational-based industries, staying ahead of the curve and adapting to new opportunities with Chat gpt as our ally can redefine the learning landscape, as exemplified by the story of educator-turned-entrepreneur, Maya.

Maya, a passionate educator, recognized the limitations of traditional teaching methods and saw the potential for technology to enhance learning experiences. Armed with this vision, she founded a startup focused on leveraging AI and machine learning to personalize education.

However, navigating the complex educational landscape presented numerous challenges. With rapidly evolving technologies and shifting pedagogical paradigms, Maya needed a reliable partner to help her anticipate trends and innovate effectively.

Enter Chat gpt, the dynamic AI companion. Maya integrated Chat gpt into her company's workflow, using its capabilities to analyze educational research, identify learner needs, and generate tailored content and strategies.

With Chat gpt's assistance, Maya's startup developed an adaptive learning platform that revolutionized the way students engage with course material. By harnessing AI-driven insights, the platform dynamically adjusted content and pacing to suit each student's learning style and proficiency level, fostering deeper understanding and retention.

One of Maya's proudest achievements was partnering with schools in underserved communities to implement the platform. By addressing individual learning needs and providing personalized support, the platform empowered students to overcome academic challenges and unlock their full potential.

The success of Maya's startup caught the attention of investors and educational institutions worldwide. With Chat gpt as her trusted advisor, Maya expanded her company's reach, establishing partnerships with schools, universities, and educational organizations globally.

Today, Maya's startup stands as a trailblazer in the educational technology sector, transforming learning outcomes and empowering learners of all backgrounds. Her journey epitomizes the transformative power of staying ahead of the curve and adapting to new opportunities with Chat gpt as our ally, reshaping education for the better and inspiring a generation of lifelong learners.

Implementing the concept of "Staying ahead of the curve and adapting to new opportunities with Chat gpt as our ally" involves several basic steps, along with the utilization of various tools to facilitate the process. Here's a breakdown of the steps and commonly used tools:

1. Identify Our Goals and Objectives: Define what we want to achieve by staying ahead of the curve and adapting to new opportunities. This could include increasing market share, expanding into new markets, or launching innovative products/services.

2. Understand Our Industry and Market Trends: Use Chat gpt to gather insights into our industry and market dynamics. Chat gpt can analyze vast amounts of data, news articles, and reports to identify emerging trends, competitor strategies, and consumer preferences.

3. Continuous Learning and Research: Stay informed about the latest advancements in our field by utilizing tools like Google Alerts, Feedly, or Pocket. These tools aggregate news articles, blog posts, and industry publications related to our interests, keeping we updated in real-time.

4. SWOT Analysis: Conduct a SWOT (Strengths, Weaknesses, Opportunities, Threats) analysis with Chat gpt's assistance to assess our company's internal capabilities and external factors affecting our business. Tools like SWOT analysis templates or platforms like Lucidchart can aid in organizing and visualizing our findings.

5. Innovation and Idea Generation: Brainstorm innovative ideas and strategies with Chat gpt to capitalize on new opportunities. Tools like Miro or Trello can facilitate collaborative ideation sessions, allowing team members to contribute and refine ideas together.

6. Strategic Planning: Develop a strategic plan based on the insights gathered with Chat gpt. Tools like Asana or Monday.com can help in creating and managing tasks, setting deadlines, and tracking progress towards our goals.

7. Agile Approach: Adopt an agile approach to adapt quickly to changing circumstances and seize new opportunities as they arise. Tools like Jira or Trello can facilitate agile project management, allowing we to prioritize tasks, collaborate with team members, and iterate on strategies efficiently.

8. Monitoring and Evaluation: Continuously monitor key performance indicators (KPIs) and evaluate the effectiveness of our strategies. Tools like Google Analytics or HubSpot provide insights into website traffic, user engagement, and marketing campaign performance, enabling data-driven decision-making.

By following these steps and leveraging tools like Chat gpt along with other supportive applications, we can effectively stay ahead of the curve, adapt to new opportunities, and drive success in our business endeavors.

IX

Useful Keywords and Commands for CHATGPT

Chat gpt, powered by OpenAI, is an advanced language model designed to generate human-like text based on the input it receives. When applied to personal advice, Chat gpt becomes a valuable tool for individuals seeking guidance on managing their concerned effectively. Whether it's budgeting, investing, debt management, or retirement planning, Chat gpt can offer insights and recommendations to help users make informed decisions about their well-being. Useful Keywords and Commands on entrepreneur journey in business development" encompass essential terms and actions crucial for entrepreneurs navigating the intricacies of business growth. These keywords and commands serve as guiding principles and practical tools to propel entrepreneurial ventures forward.

Keywords such as "market research" illuminate the importance of understanding target audiences, industry trends, and competitive landscapes. Entrepreneurs employ this knowledge to identify market gaps and opportunities, laying the groundwork for strategic decision-making.

"Strategic planning" emphasizes the necessity of formulating clear objectives, defining actionable strategies, and outlining measurable milestones. This process enables entrepreneurs to chart a course for sustainable growth and adapt to changing market dynamics effectively.

"Networking" underscores the significance of building relationships with industry peers, mentors, and potential collaborators. Leveraging networks fosters opportunities for partnerships, knowledge exchange, and access to resources critical for business development.

"Innovation" highlights the role of creativity and forward-thinking in driving competitive advantage and differentiation. Entrepreneurs constantly seek innovative solutions, products, or processes to meet evolving consumer needs and disrupt existing markets.

Commands such as "analyze data" emphasize the importance of leveraging data analytics tools to extract actionable insights from customer feedback, sales metrics, and market trends. Data-driven decision-making enables entrepreneurs to optimize strategies, minimize risks, and capitalize on emerging opportunities.

Useful Keywords and Commands for Chat gpt in Emotional Intelligence

1. Emotion Recognition: "Identify the predominant emotion expressed in this message."

2. Empathetic Response Generation: "Generate an empathetic response to someone expressing sadness."

3. Conflict Resolution Strategies: "Provide strategies for resolving a conflict with a colleague."

4. Active Listening Techniques: "Offer tips for practicing active listening in conversations."

5. Empathy Building Exercises: "Recommend exercises for building empathy and understanding towards others."

6. Validation Statements: "Suggest validation statements to acknowledge someone's feelings."

7. Stress Management Techniques: "Share techniques for managing stress and anxiety in challenging situations."

8. Mindfulness Practices: "Recommend mindfulness practices for cultivating emotional awareness and resilience."

9. Communication Skills Development: "Provide guidance on improving communication skills, especially in sensitive conversations."

10. Self-Reflection Prompts: "Offer prompts for self-reflection on personal emotions and experiences."

11. Boundary Setting Strategies: "Advise on setting healthy boundaries in relationships and interactions."

12. Gratitude Practices: "Share exercises for cultivating gratitude and positive emotions."

13. Coping Strategies for Difficult Emotions: "Recommend coping strategies for dealing with anger or frustration."

14. Assertiveness Training: "Offer techniques for assertive communication in difficult conversations."

15. Trauma-Informed Support: "Provide trauma-informed support strategies for interacting with individuals who have experienced trauma."

16. Emotional Regulation Techniques: "Share techniques for regulating and managing strong emotions."

17. Social Skills Development: "Recommend resources for improving social skills and building meaningful connections."

18. Vulnerability Sharing Guidelines: "Offer guidelines for sharing vulnerabilities and fostering trust in relationships."

19. Compassion Cultivation Practices: "Recommend practices for cultivating compassion towards oneself and others."

20. De-escalation Strategies: "Provide strategies for de-escalating tense situations and diffusing conflict."

Commands for Interacting with Chat gpt Virtual Assistants:

1. "Can you schedule a meeting for me?"

2. "Remind me to submit the report by tomorrow."

3. "Find nearby restaurants that serve Italian cuisine."

4. "What's the weather forecast for tomorrow?"

5. "Book a flight to New York for next week."

6. "Set an alarm for 7:00 AM."

7. "Order groceries for delivery."

8. "Translate 'hello' into French."

9. "Calculate the tip for a $50 bill."

10. "Tell me a joke."

Commands for Interacting with Chat gpt for Content Creation:

1. "Generate ideas for a blog post about digital marketing trends."

2. "Help me draft an introduction for an article on artificial intelligence."

3. "Expand on the benefits of using renewable energy sources."

4. "Suggest SEO keywords for optimizing a product description."

5. "Create a catchy headline for a social media post about healthy eating."

6. "Summarize recent research findings on climate change."

7. "Craft a product description for a new line of eco-friendly skincare products."

8. "Generate creative content for an email marketing campaign."

9. "Translate this blog post into Spanish."

10. "Write a short story based on the prompt 'lost in a mysterious forest'."

Commands for Engaging Chat gpt for Mental Health Support:

1. "I'm feeling anxious. Can we help me calm down?"

2. "How can I cope with stress more effectively?"

3. "I'm struggling with depression. What should I do?"

4. "Can you recommend mindfulness exercises for relaxation?"

5. "I'm having suicidal thoughts. What should I do?"

6. "Provide tips for improving my self-esteem."

7. "I'm experiencing symptoms of PTSD. Can we offer support?"

8. "How can I set boundaries in my relationships to protect my mental health?"

9. "Can you recommend self-help books for managing anxiety?"

10. "I need to talk to someone. Can we listen?"

Commands for Chat gpt in Healthcare:

1. "What are the symptoms of [medical condition]?"

2. "How can I prevent [medical condition]?"

3. "What are the treatment options for [medical condition]?"

4. "Can you help me schedule an appointment with Dr. [provider name]?"

5. "What are the side effects of [medication name]?"

6. "Remind me to take my medication at [time]."

7. "What is my next appointment with Dr. [provider name]?"

8. "How do I check my blood pressure using a home monitor?"

9. "Can you recommend healthy recipes for [dietary restriction]?"

10. "How can I improve my sleep quality?"

11. "What is telemedicine and how does it work?"

12. "What are the benefits of regular exercise?"

13. "What should I do in case of a medical emergency?"

14. "How can I manage my stress levels?"

15. "Can you provide information about COVID-19 vaccines?"

16. "What are the risk factors for heart disease?"

17. "How do I interpret the results of my blood tests?"

18. "Can you recommend a specialist for [specific medical condition]?"

19. "How do I find a pharmacy near me?"

20. "What is the cost of [medical procedure]?"

Most Important Commands for Chat gpt for Legal Assistance:

1. "What are my rights in [specific legal situation]?"

2. "Can you explain the terms of this contract to me?"

3. "How do I file for divorce in [jurisdiction]?"

4. "Can you help me draft a lease agreement for a rental property?"

5. "What are the steps to start a small claims court case?"

6. "How do I dispute a traffic ticket?"

7. "What are the legal requirements for creating a will?"

8. "Can we provide guidance on child custody arrangements?"

9. "What are my options for resolving a landlord-tenant dispute?"

10. "How do I respond to a lawsuit?"

11. "What are the grounds for a legal appeal?"

12. "Can you help me understand the terms of this insurance policy?"

13. "How do I protect my intellectual property rights?"

14. "What are the legal consequences of breach of contract?"

15. "Can you recommend a lawyer specializing in [specific area of law]?"

16. "How do I obtain a restraining order?"

17. "What are the steps to form a business entity?"

18. "Can you provide legal advice on a real estate transaction?"

19. "What are my rights as a tenant?"

20. "How do I enforce a court judgment?"

Commands for Chat gpt Personal Finance Advice

1. Budgeting Assistance: "Help me create a monthly budget."

2. Debt Management: "How can I effectively pay off my credit card debt?"

3. Investment Advice: "What are some good investment options for someone with a moderate risk tolerance?"

4. Retirement Planning: "How much should I be saving for retirement each month?"

5. Emergency Fund Guidance: "How much should I have in my emergency fund?"

6. Tax Strategies: "What are some tax-saving strategies I can implement?"

7. Insurance Recommendations: "What types of insurance do I need and how much coverage should I have?"

8. Financial Goal Setting: "How can I set and prioritize my financial goals?"

9. Savings Strategies: "What are some effective strategies for saving money?"

10. Credit Score Improvement: "How can I improve my credit score?"

11. Investment Diversification: "Why is diversification important in investing, and how can I achieve it?"

12. Real Estate Advice: "Should I rent or buy a home, considering my financial situation?"

13. Student Loan Management: "What options do I have for managing my student loan debt?"

14. Side Income Ideas: "What are some legitimate ways to earn extra income on the side?"

15. Financial Risk Assessment: "How can I assess and mitigate financial risks?"

16. Comparison Shopping: "How can I find the best deals on major purchases like electronics or appliances?"

17. Estate Planning: "What steps should I take to plan my estate and ensure my assets are distributed according to my wishes?"

18. Identity Theft Protection: "How can I protect myself from identity theft and fraud?"

19. Financial Health Check-Up: "Can you evaluate my current financial situation and suggest areas for improvement?"

20. Long-Term Wealth Building: "What strategies can I use to build wealth over the long term?"

Most important Commands for Chat gpt in Chatbot Development

1. Intent Recognition: "Identify the user's intent based on their message."

2. Entity Extraction: "Extract relevant entities from the user's input, such as names, dates, or locations."

3. Response Generation: "Generate a response to the user's query or statement."

4. Context Management: "Maintain context across multiple turns of conversation to ensure coherent dialogue flow."

5. Fallback Handling: "Handle situations where the chatbot is unable to understand or provide a relevant response."

6. Multimodal Interaction: "Integrate text, images, or other media formats into the chatbot's responses."

7. User Engagement Metrics: "Track metrics such as user engagement, session duration, and completion rate to evaluate chatbot performance."

8. User Authentication: "Authenticate users and manage user sessions within the chatbot environment."

9. Integration with APIs: "Integrate external APIs to provide access to third-party services or information within the chatbot."

10. Conversation History Retrieval: "Retrieve and review the conversation history to provide personalized responses based on past interactions."

11. Language Translation: "Support language translation capabilities to enable multilingual conversations with users."

12. Emotion Detection: "Detect and respond to the user's emotions expressed in their messages."

13. Content Moderation: "Implement content moderation features to filter out inappropriate or offensive user input."

14. User Profiling: "Create and update user profiles to personalize the chatbot's responses and recommendations."

15. Question Answering: "Answer factual questions or provide information based on the user's inquiries."

16. Task Automation: "Automate repetitive tasks or workflows through the chatbot interface."

17. Feedback Collection: "Collect user feedback to identify areas for improvement and enhance the chatbot's performance."

18. Error Handling: "Handle errors gracefully and provide helpful error messages to guide users through troubleshooting steps."

19. User Onboarding: "Guide new users through the chatbot's features and functionalities to ensure a smooth onboarding experience."

20. Continuous Training: "Continuously train and update the chatbot with new data to improve its language understanding and response generation capabilities."

Most important Commands for Chat gpt in Personal Productivity

1. Task Creation: "Create a new task for me to complete today."

2. Priority Setting: "Help me prioritize my tasks for the day."

3. Time Blocking: "Recommend time-blocking strategies to manage my schedule more effectively."

4. Deadline Reminder: "Set a reminder for me to complete a task by a specific deadline."

5. Productivity Tips: "Share some productivity tips to help me stay focused and motivated."

6. Goal Setting: "Assist me in setting SMART goals for the upcoming month."

7. Progress Tracking: "Provide an overview of my progress towards my current goals."

8. Distraction Management: "Offer advice on how to minimize distractions and stay productive."

9. Pomodoro Technique: "Explain how to use the Pomodoro Technique for time management."

10. Project Management: "Suggest project management tools to help me organize my tasks and deadlines."

11. Daily Reflection: "Guide me through a daily reflection exercise to review my accomplishments and areas for improvement."

12. Break Schedule: "Recommend an optimal schedule for taking breaks throughout the day."

13. Mindfulness Exercises: "Share mindfulness exercises to help me reduce stress and improve focus."

14. Email Management: "Provide tips for managing and organizing my email inbox more efficiently."

15. Routine Optimization: "Help me optimize my daily routine for maximum productivity."

16. Batch Processing: "Explain the concept of batch processing and how it can improve efficiency."

17. Digital Detox Strategies: "Suggest strategies for taking regular digital detox breaks to recharge."

18. Self-Care Practices: "Recommend self-care practices to maintain physical and mental well-being."

19. Learning and Skill Development: "Provide resources and recommendations for continuous learning and skill development."

20. Reflective Journaling: "Guide me through a reflective journaling exercise to track my personal growth and achievements."

Most important Commands for Chat gpt in Agriculture

1. Crop Recommendations: "Recommend suitable crops for cultivation in my region based on soil type and climate conditions."

2. Pest Identification: "Identify the pest causing damage to my crops and suggest control measures."

3. Weather Forecast: "Provide a weather forecast for the upcoming week to assist in farm planning."

4. Soil Health Assessment: "Assess the health of my soil and recommend amendments to improve fertility."

5. Irrigation Optimization: "Optimize irrigation scheduling to minimize water usage and maximize crop yield."

6. Disease Management: "Offer strategies for managing a fungal disease affecting my tomato plants."

7. Crop Rotation Planning: "Advise on crop rotation practices to maintain soil health and prevent disease buildup."

8. Livestock Nutrition: "Recommend a balanced diet for my dairy cows to optimize milk production."

9. Breeding Strategies: "Provide guidance on selecting breeding pairs for genetic improvement of my poultry flock."

10. Market Analysis: "Conduct a market analysis to identify profitable crops or livestock products for sale."

11. Agroforestry Design: "Design an agroforestry system for my farm to promote biodiversity and ecosystem services."

12. Drought Management: "Suggest drought-resistant crop varieties and water-saving techniques for coping with water scarcity."

13. Precision Agriculture: "Implement precision agriculture techniques for variable rate application of inputs based on field variability."

14. Organic Farming Practices: "Recommend organic farming practices for transitioning my farm to organic certification."

15. Integrated Pest Management (IPM): "Develop an integrated pest management plan for controlling pests in my vineyard."

16. Carbon Sequestration Strategies: "Propose strategies for enhancing carbon sequestration on my farm to mitigate climate change."

17. Greenhouse Gas Emissions Reduction: "Identify opportunities to reduce greenhouse gas emissions from livestock production."

18. Agricultural Policy Analysis: "Analyze current agricultural policies and their impact on small-scale farmers in my region."

19. Post-Harvest Handling: "Provide guidelines for post-harvest handling and storage of my grain crops to prevent spoilage."

20. Farm Business Planning: "Assist in developing a business plan for diversifying my farm income through agritourism activities."

Most Important Commands for Chat gpt in Mental Wellness Coaching:

1. "I'm feeling overwhelmed. Can you help me calm down?"

2. "What are some relaxation techniques I can use to reduce stress?"

3. "Can you provide tips for improving my sleep quality?"

4. "How do I practice mindfulness meditation?"

5. "What are the signs of burnout, and how can I prevent it?"

6. "Help me develop a self-care routine."

7. "I'm struggling with negative thoughts. How can I challenge them?"

8. "Recommend resources for coping with anxiety."

9. "Provide strategies for setting boundaries in relationships."

10. "How do I build resilience in the face of adversity?"

11. "What are healthy ways to cope with loneliness?"

12. "Suggest activities for boosting my mood."

13. "Can you explain the benefits of journaling for mental health?"

14. "How do I recognize signs of depression in myself or others?"

15. "Help me create a plan for managing my workload and avoiding burnout."

16. "Recommend self-help books for personal growth and well-being."

17. "What are some effective ways to manage anger?"

18. "Can you provide guidance on improving self-esteem?"

19. "I'm experiencing relationship issues. What should I do?"

20. "Help me find a therapist or counselor in my area."

Most Important Commands for Chat gpt in Parenting Support:

1. "How can I manage my toddler's temper tantrums?"

2. "Provide tips for fostering positive sibling relationships."

3. "What are age-appropriate activities for my preschooler?"

4. "How do I establish a bedtime routine for my child?"

5. "Can you recommend strategies for effective discipline?"

6. "What are the signs of developmental milestones in infants?"

7. "Discuss the importance of positive reinforcement in parenting."

8. "How can I promote healthy eating habits in my child?"

9. "Provide guidance on managing screen time for children."

10. "What are effective ways to communicate with teenagers?"

11. "Discuss the impact of divorce on children and coping strategies."

12. "How do I address my child's academic challenges?"

13. "What are the benefits of outdoor play for children?"

14. "Can you recommend resources for parenting books or podcasts?"

15. "How do I handle bullying situations involving my child?"

16. "Discuss strategies for fostering emotional intelligence in children."

17. "What are effective ways to manage parent-child conflicts?"

18. "Provide tips for building resilience in children."

19. "How can I support my child's social-emotional development?"

20. "Discuss the importance of self-care for parents."

Most Important Commands for Chat gpt in Personality Assessment:

1. "Assess my personality based on my writing style."

2. "What are my dominant personality traits?"

3. "Provide insights into my communication style."

4. "Am I an introvert or an extrovert?"

5. "Assess my emotional intelligence."

6. "What are my strengths and weaknesses?"

7. "Suggest career paths that align with my personality."

8. "Do I exhibit traits of conscientiousness?"

9. "Am I more analytical or creative in my thinking?"

10. "Assess my level of openness to new experiences."

11. "What motivates me in life?"

12. "Evaluate my levels of agreeableness and empathy."

13. "Provide insights into my leadership potential."

14. "Am I prone to stress or anxiety?"

15. "Assess my levels of resilience and adaptability."

16. "Do I exhibit traits of optimism or pessimism?"

17. "Suggest strategies for improving my communication skills."

18. "Assess my levels of assertiveness and confidence."

19. "Provide insights into my decision-making style."

20. "Recommend personal development exercises or activities."

CASE STUDIES

Case Study 1; Sarah, an aspiring entrepreneur, used CHAT GPT to brainstorm business ideas. By engaging in conversational prompts , she explored various industries and identified a gap in the market for eco-friendly household products.Sarah founded her own company, offering sustainable alternatives to everyday essentials.

Case Study 2: Mark's Journey Mark, a tech enthusiast, wanted to start his own software company but was unsure of which product to develop. Using CHAT GPT, he generated multiple ideas and received feedback on their feasibility. After validating potential ideas through market research, Mark decided to create a productivity app tailored for remote workers. The app gained traction quickly.

Case Study 3: Aarya's Experience Aarya, an entrepreneur in the fashion industry, sought to expand her business into new markets. She analyzed consumer behavior, competitor strategies, and emerging trends in the fashion industry. This data-driven approach guided Aarya in launching a new line of sustainable clothing, catering to environmentally conscious consumers. The market insights provided by CHAT GPT helped Aarya make informed decisions that led to the success of her expansion efforts.

Case Study 4: David, an aspiring restaurateur, used CHAT GPT to draft his business plan , he articulated his vision, identified target demographics, and outlined marketing strategies. The comprehensive business plan, refined with feedback, impressed investors and secured funding for David's restaurant venture. Today, his restaurant is thriving.

Case Study 5: Lisa's Branding Journey- Lisa, a startup founder, leveraged CHAT GPT to develop her brand identity. Through conversational prompts, she defined her brand values, voice, and messaging. It generated creative content, including taglines and brand stories, that resonated with Lisa's vision. With a cohesive brand identity established , Lisa successfully launched her business and attracted a loyal customer base.

Case Study 6 Alex's Automation Strategy , a small business owner, integrated CHAT GPT into his customer service operations. By deploying a chatbot powered , Alex automated responses to frequently asked questions and customer inquiries. This not only improved response times but also freed up staff to focus on more complex tasks. With CHAT GPT handling routine queries efficiently, Alex's business experienced increased customer satisfaction and operational efficiency.

Case Study 7: Emma's Customer-Centric Approach Emma, an e-commerce entrepreneur, implemented CHAT GPT-powered chatbots on her website to enhance customer engagement. These chatbots provided personalized product recommendations, answered customer queries, and facilitated seamless transactions.

Case Study 8: Michael's Growth Strategy- Michael, the founder of a tech startup, utilized CHAT GPT to scale his business operations., he automated lead generation, streamlined project management, and optimized marketing campaigns. This allowed Michael to expand his customer base and enter new markets efficiently. Michael's startup achieved sustainable scalability and long-term success.

Case Study 9: Sarah's Data-Driven Approach - Sarah, a business consultant, to analyze market data and trends for her clients. Sarah obtained actionable insights and recommendations. Armed with CHAT GPT's analysis, Sarah helped her clients make informed decisions that resulted in increased profitability and competitive advantage in their respective industries.

Case Study 10: James' Forward-Thinking Vision - James, a forward-thinking entrepreneur, He continually explored new ways to leverage CHAT GPT's evolving capabilities, such as predictive analytics and natural language understanding, to stay ahead of the competition , James positioned his business for future success in a rapidly changing landscape.

Success story of Entrepreneurs

1. Priya's Story: Priya , a stay-at-home mom with a passion for baking, used CHAT GPT to explore potential business ideas. Through conversations, she discovered a niche market for organic, allergen-free baked goods.

Inspired by this insight, Priya launched her own online bakery, which quickly gained popularity among health-conscious consumers.

2. Mark's Journey: Mark, a recent college graduate, wanted to start his own tech company but was unsure where to begin. Using CHAT GPT, he researched various industries and identified a gap in the market for mobile applications catering to mental health. Mark developed an app that provides users with personalized self-care tips and resources, ultimately transforming his idea into a successful business venture.

3. Maryam's Experience: Maryam, a fashion enthusiast, dreamed of starting her own clothing brand. CHAT GPT's assistance, she conducted market research to identify consumer preferences and emerging trends in the fashion industry. Armed with valuable insights, Maryam launched her brand, offering affordable, sustainable clothing options that resonated with environmentally conscious consumers.

4. David's Success: David, an aspiring restaurateur, used CHAT GPT to draft a comprehensive business plan for his restaurant concept. It helped him outline his vision, define target demographics, and develop marketing strategies. With a solid plan in hand, David With secured funding from investors and successfully opened his restaurant, which quickly became a local favorite.

5. Lisa's Branding Journey: Lisa, a graphic designer turned entrepreneur, leveraged CHAT GPT to develop her brand identity. Through conversational prompts, she defined her brand values, voice, and messaging, Lisa crafted a compelling brand story and visual identity that set her business apart in a competitive market, leading to increased brand recognition and customer loyalty.

6. Michael's Innovation Strategy: Michael, a tech entrepreneur, used CHAT GPT to brainstorm ideas for his next startup venture. he explored various industries and identified opportunities in the healthcare sector. After validating potential ideas through market research, Michael founded a telemedicine platform that connects patients with healthcare providers online, filling a critical need in the market.

7. Rachel's Product Development Journey: Rachel, a product manager at a tech company, utilized CHAT GPT to generate ideas for new product features. she conducted user surveys and analyzed customer feedback to identify pain points and opportunities for innovation. Rachel then collaborated with her team to develop and launch new features that addressed user needs and enhanced the overall user experience.

8. John's Startup Pivot: John, the founder of a struggling startup, turned to CHAT GPT for guidance on pivoting his business model. Through conversations with , he explored alternative markets and revenue streams. John successfully pivoted his startup to focus on a new target audience, leading to renewed growth and profitability.

9.Maria's Market Expansion Strategy: Maria, the owner of a small retail business, used CHAT GPT to explore opportunities for expanding into new markets. By analyzing data and trends, she identified promising locations and demographics for expansion. Armed with this information, Maria opened new storefronts in strategic locations, effectively growing her customer base and revenue.

10.Thomas' Entrepreneurial Journey: Thomas, a recent college graduate, leveraged CHAT GPT to explore potential business ideas. By engaging in conversations with, he discovered a passion for sustainable agriculture and identified a market opportunity for organic produce delivery services., Thomas launched his own farm-to-table delivery service, which quickly gained traction among health-conscious consumers in his community.

Afterword

As we reach the conclusion of "How to Use ChatGPT to Become a Successful Entrepreneur: 9 Secret Steps Which Make You a Billionaire," I hope you now feel equipped with the knowledge and confidence to harness the power of ChatGPT in your entrepreneurial journey. This book has aimed to provide you with not only the technical know-how but also the strategic insights to leverage AI for unprecedented business growth. The nine steps outlined in this book are designed to be practical, actionable, and transformative. They reflect the potential of integrating ChatGPT into various aspects of your business—from automating mundane tasks and generating creative content to enhancing customer interactions and making data-driven decisions. These steps are your toolkit for navigating the complex and ever-evolving landscape of modern entrepreneurship.

Remember, the journey to success is not a sprint but a marathon. The integration of AI into your business processes is an ongoing effort that requires continuous learning, adaptation, and innovation. Stay curious, remain open to new ideas, and never stop exploring the possibilities that technology offers.

I encourage you to revisit the principles and strategies discussed here regularly and to adapt them to your unique circumstances and business environment. The true measure of success lies not just in achieving financial milestones but in creating lasting impact and value.

Thank you for embarking on this journey with me. May your entrepreneurial ventures be filled with innovation, growth, and boundless success. Here's to your future as a

pioneering entrepreneur and, perhaps, a billionaire.
To your continued success,
NEHAL AHMAD

Epilogue

As we close this journey through "How to Use ChatGPT to Become a Successful Entrepreneur: 9 Secret Steps Which Make You a Billionaire," reflect on the incredible potential at your fingertips. The integration of AI, particularly ChatGPT, into your business is not just a strategy—it's a paradigm shift that can propel you to new heights of success. The nine steps we've explored are designed to be your roadmap, guiding you through innovative ways to optimize your business operations, engage with customers, and make data-driven decisions. Embrace these strategies with an open mind and a spirit of continuous learning.

Your entrepreneurial journey is just beginning. With determination, creativity, and the powerful tool of ChatGPT, you have the potential to transform your business and achieve extraordinary success.

Thank you for embarking on this journey. Here's to your future as a visionary entrepreneur and, perhaps, a billionaire.

To your success,
Nehal Ahmad

9 7 9 8 8 9 4 7 5 7 5 5 1